Praise for *Refuse to Be 1*

"Matt Bell reminds us that beyond inspiration lies attentiveness, craft, and revision, revision, revision. *Refuse to Be Done* is a guide to fiction writing so full of beautifully expressed practical advice, touching on everything from what to write, to how and when to write, that it's, truly, viscerally exciting to read. Perhaps improbably, Bell is as masterly a writer about fiction as he is a writer of fiction. I can't imagine anyone setting pen to paper, or fingertips to keyboard, who won't want to keep this book permanently close at hand."   **—Benjamin Dreyer,**
New York Times bestselling author of *Dreyer's English*

"Drawing on the wisdom of everyone from Ursula K. Le Guin to The Pixies, plus his own successes and struggles, Matt Bell has given the world a tremendously clear (but never over-prescriptive) guide to the wonderful mess of writing a novel. I want this book in my students' hands yesterday; I'm grateful to hold it in mine today."   **—Rebecca Makkai,**
Pulitzer Finalist for *The Great Believers*

"Matt Bell has written an essential, passionate guide to the art of the novel. What makes this such an excellent primer is how Bell anchors everything in writing as an act of discovery. He ties that discovery to the practice of revising and listening to your work. And he gives concrete, technical suggestions on how to do that without sacrificing sophistication and without resorting to formulas. A gift to writers at any level."

—Dana Spiotta,
National Book Award Finalist for *Eat the Document*

"Matt Bell's brilliant *Refuse to Be Done* offers writers and writing teachers everywhere a clear guide to a process that seems daunting to me still: how to organize the writing and revision of a novel? How to avoid having 740 drafts labeled 'final'? How to make a best effort and let it fly? There's so much art in this, and so much art will come of it. Essential for newbies and old hands alike." —**Alexander Chee, Whiting Award–winning author of *How to Write an Autobiographical Novel***

"This is the CrossFit of craft books, a literary piece of gym equipment that will help you progress dynamically through your creative projects with agency, clear-sightedness, and a new appreciation for the often overlooked, but utterly essential act—and art—of revision. *Refuse to Be Done* is a must-have for the writer who is ready to up their writing game."
—**Courtney Maum, author of *Before and After the Book Deal: A Writer's Guide to Finishing, Publishing, Promoting and Surviving Your First Book***

"*Refuse to Be Done* isn't merely a book on how to write a novel, it's also a book on how to be a writer, how to think like a person whose book will be on a shelf. We used to be told to kill our darlings, but I don't think that's true anymore, not after reading Matt's excellent advice. If we do as he tells us, our darlings might just grow up and move out on their own, never to bother us again . . . until the next time we find ourselves staring at that blank page. A book perfect for the newcomer or the seasoned author who needs a fresh way to look at the novel."
—**Tod Goldberg, *New York Times* bestselling author of *Gangsterland***

REFUSE TO BE DONE

How to Write and Rewrite a Novel in Three Drafts

ALSO BY MATT BELL

Done

*How to Write and Rewrite
a Novel in Three Drafts*

MATT BELL

SOHO

Published by
Soho Press, Inc.
227 W 17th Street
New York, NY 10011

Library of Congress Cataloging-in-Publication Data

Names: Bell, Matt, author.
Title: Refuse to be done : how to write
and rewrite a novel in three drafts / Matt Bell.
Description: New York : Soho, [2022]
Identifiers: LCCN 2021046774

ISBN 978-1-64129-341-9
eISBN 978-1-64129-342-6

Subjects: LCSH: Fiction—Authorship. | Fiction—Technique.
Classification: LCC PN3365 .B46 2022 | DDC 808.3—dc23/eng/20211006
LC record available at https://lccn.loc.gov/2021046774

Interior design by Janine Agro, Soho Press, Inc.

Printed in the United States of America

10 9 8 7

To Anne Valente, Callista Buchen, Dustin M. Hoffman,
Gregory Howard, and Joseph Scapellato, with thanks

Writing a novel is kind of like scaling Mt. Everest and passing by your own bones on the way.

—Karen Russell

INTRODUCTION:

The Three Drafts

You are writing a novel. You are writing a book.

Go ahead and tell yourself. And then tell yourself again.

Maybe say it a few more times, for luck.

No matter what phase in the process you're in when you read this page—whether you're already laboring on your novel, whether you've not yet written a word—I implore you to continually affirm that you are writing a novel, that you are writing a book. Don't diminish, don't equivocate, don't find some way to keep from claiming the work.

If only to yourself, if only in the tiniest whisper, say it: *I am writing a novel.*

If it's the first time you've ever said this to yourself, I hope it feels good. If you've been saying it for years already, I hope it's a rededication of your commitment to a pursuit to which you've likely already dedicated many long hours. But what is it that you're doing, exactly, when you're writing a novel, filling the hours spent at your desk? Maybe your focus is on telling a gripping story, or bringing great characters to life, or plotting intricate mysteries, or inventing new worlds, or exploring family dramas, or capturing the stream-of-consciousness thoughts of one particular person as precisely as possible. Whatever your primary aim is for your novel, it doesn't on its own tell you what the task of going from the empty page to a finished manuscript will look like, in practical terms.

This book is one attempt to fill in that blank, by offering actionable steps for every phase of the process as it applies to many of the kinds of novels being written and published today.

Samuel R. Delany once said that "eighty-five to ninety-five percent of my work is rewriting and revision." That's been my experience, too, although I didn't always recognize it. As a student, I took years of creative writing workshops, and in most of those workshops, I was required to turn in an end-of-the-semester revision, demonstrating how I'd worked with the feedback I'd received from my classmates and my teachers. But requiring students to revise isn't the same as teaching students *how* to do it. In the absence of strategy, I relied on brute repetition to improve my stories: I wrote draft after draft, covering printed pages in red ink before returning to the computer to input countless changes I was never sure were necessarily improvements.

Given sufficient time and a lot of effort, I was able to bully many of my rough drafts into respectable submissions and, then, with the help of kind editors, into readable stories capable of being printed in magazines and books. But when I started writing novels, I realized that as hard as short stories had been to revise, rewriting a novel draft of three hundred pages or so was far more daunting—and that would've been the case even if my first novel draft hadn't come out more broken than my average short story.

Over the years, I've come to believe that revision and rewriting are most of what good writing entails: writing a successful book isn't only making the most of the first burst of inspiration, as pleasurable as that is. It's also the sustained and often small-scale work of making a promising manuscript better hour by hour, day by day, slowly but steadily moving it closer to your imagined ideal. So, while this is theoretically a book about revision, it's also a step-by-step guide to writing a novel—and because I believe rewriting and revision necessarily occur at every stage of the process, I've organized this guide into three large chapters, each devoted to one of what I think of as the "three drafts."

You might be reading this book with a blank page in front of you, or with a partial draft already under way. In either case, you can employ the tactics in the "First Draft" chapter to practice *generative revision*, the kind of rewriting that will help you continue drafting and eventually finish the first version of your novel. This is where you'll find tactics for sustaining and extending your story and for overcoming common road-blocks and frustrations. At this stage, I advocate an exploratory, organic, and above all playful approach, not because it's the only way to draft a novel, but because it's the most enjoyable way I know how.

When I finished the earliest draft of what would become my first published novel, I realized I didn't know how to approach improving so much material at once. The strategies in the "Second Draft" chapter emerged from my need to shape the rough, unwieldy material of a first draft toward a better-made, better-plotted second, which I did by a process I'll call *narrative revision*, because the big decisions you'll make during this draft will be about how to restructure and rewrite the dramatic material of the story to maximal effect. In many ways, this is the hardest turn to make, but it's also one of the more fulfilling parts of the process, as it's the stage where you'll make the most significant improvements to your plot, transforming your novel from *draft* to *book*.

In the "Third Draft" chapter, you'll find a layered approach to "final" edits, where you'll ensure, by a series of smaller and more workable tasks, that your now well-structured, well-plotted book is as enjoyable as possible. You can think of this stage as *polishing revision*, but you might plan to make dramatic changes here, too.

You may already have noticed that this first-draft, second-draft, third-draft structure is rather tidy. These "drafts" might be easier to think of as "stages," with the understanding that you might linger in one stage for a long time and then breeze through another; you might also return to a previous stage's strategies at any time or repeat a stage more than once, if necessary. More than likely, at certain points in the work, you'll find yourself employing strategies from all three stages at once.

Because of this, there's no one right way to read this book: if you're starting from scratch, you might move through this book in a linear fashion, but I hope you'll also feel free to try the revision tactics ahead in whatever order you wish, adapting my process to yours.

TAKE ONLY WHAT'S USEFUL

The novel-writing process described in this book is a version of my own, and therefore it necessarily proceeds from my personal preferences regarding craft, audience, and story. (It also most likely re-creates my blind spots, although I've done my best to address those where I can; one goal of all good teachers has to be not to pass on their own lacks to their students.) While my own novels have been promoted as literary fiction of the speculative, genre-hopping variety, my interests as a reader and a student of craft are more varied and wide-ranging and, I hope, are getting more so every year. I worked at a small publishing house for several years, where I edited novels by writers working in a variety of styles, and for the past decade I've been teaching novel writing to students with unique goals, aesthetics, and intended audiences, all of which I try my best to honor and encourage in our working together.

All this is only to say that while I believe much of what I suggest ahead will work for many different kinds of fiction writers, it's more than okay if certain tactics or techniques don't work for you or feel at cross-purposes with the kind of novel you want to write. The aim of this book isn't to make anyone into the kind of novelist I am—anything but that!—but to help you become more yourself, on the page and throughout your process. So, if some of the forthcoming advice doesn't feel like it applies to your novel, go ahead and discard what doesn't help or, better yet, subvert it: there's as much to be gained by actively opposing a craft lesson as there is in following it.

This book is here to serve you and *your* book. Only what's useful to you applies.

FIRST DRAFT:
Forward Progress, Generative Revision

Now that we're ready to begin, you might ask: What kind of first draft am I suggesting you should write?

The quick answer: whatever kind you can. Whatever gets you through, whatever puts a beginning, middle, and end down on paper.

My longer answer is that you should aim to write what I call an *exploratory draft.*

Here's how I do it. As I set out to begin a new novel, I usually start without a formal outline. While I'm planning to finish with a well-structured plot, I've never been able to start there; in fact, I sometimes have only the slightest inkling of what the story might be or who the characters are. For me, knowing too much detail in advance hems me in, tying my hands and stifling my imagination. In the earliest days of drafting, I'm often working in fragments of language and disconnected images, partial scenes and half conversations and unordered events.

Why indulge in such chaos? Because what I'm trying to do

in the first draft is to *discover* the book I'm writing *by writing the book*.

What I've found is that overplanning before beginning writing risks blocking opportunities for discovery and surprise. Rather than dutifully following an outline, I want to be guided by what appears on the page as I write, by the emerging desires of characters and the dramatic demands of drafted scenes as well as by the acoustics of my sentences and the possibilities of the narrator's voice. Following any individual writing day's whims and interests, I pay attention for inspiration filtering in from my daily life and from the books I'm reading and other media I'm consuming. Then I try to put that inspiration to work in my draft, letting it flourish where it will.

I'm not the only writer who proceeds in this way. Of his own drafts, Robert Boswell writes, "I come to know my stories by writing my way into them. I focus on the characters without trying to attach significance to their actions. I do not look for symbols. For as long as I can, I remain purposely blind to the machinery of the story and only partially cognizant of the world the story creates . . . [B]y declining to analyze the story, I hope to keep it open to surprise." Similarly, Heidi Julavits says, "I don't think out the plot ahead of time . . . I would feel like I was an architect executing a blueprint. If I'd done the discovery before I wrote the book, then there would be nothing to discover. It would feel dutiful instead of exciting."

How does this work in practice? I wrote for a month on my novel *Scrapper* before learning my protagonist's name. I had the title before I started, but not the character: I knew only that I wanted to write about the illegal metal scrapping industry in the abandoned buildings of Detroit. So, I knew my protagonist's occupation but not who he was; by writing scenes in which he plied his trade, I learned what he cared about, what he desired, what he feared. A month in, I discovered the novel's true inciting incident—a kidnapped boy, held in an abandoned house, who needed saving—by moving my protagonist through Detroit's urban landscape, keeping him active, and paying attention to what he noticed in the places I sent him, with *what he noticed* being the details I invented to fill out the scenes I was discovering alongside him.

I don't know what novel I would have written if I'd outlined *Scrapper* in advance, but I know it wouldn't have been the novel I eventually published.

I know this can sound a little magical: *start writing, and the draft will come*. It will come, but I understand your not taking my word for it. In the pages that follow, I'll suggest some practical ways of ensuring that it does by creating your own exploratory experience of discovery. But if you feel more comfortable writing an outline before you begin, I won't stop you: It's your book! Outline away. (Chapter 2 covers some planning techniques you might try.) But don't let whatever outline you make become a straitjacket. For me, a process like Nicholson Baker's sounds ideal: "I sometimes make an ordered sequence of scenes and observations I want to include, before I start writing, but I don't follow it," Baker says. "The right order only comes when I'm in the middle of a paragraph, groping, wearing the miner's hat, and looking around for where to totter off to next."

Whether you write a full outline or make a list of scenes or paste hand-scrawled index cards all over your office wall, the important thing is not to let any of these organization schemes constrain you too early. One of the surest dangers a novel faces in its early life is a writer too eager to be sure of what it is. Pay attention to your own desires, but listen to the pages you're accumulating: as you play on, writing your story, sooner or later the pages begin to play back. That's the moment a draft comes to life, if you'll give it room to breathe. Much of what I'll suggest in this chapter is about how you reach that stage with as much possibility and surprise left on the table as you can.

REMEMBER: TODAY'S TASK IS NEVER TO WRITE A BOOK

Rachel Kushner once said that the writing of her first novel, *Telex from Cuba*, "was characterized by an enduring oscillation between perseverance and a profound doubt." This seems to be a pretty common sentiment among novelists, and so you may already have experienced this oscillation yourself. One thing to do from the very beginning of your draft, then, is to create stores of perseverance and confidence you can draw on whenever those doubts rear their heads.

In the introduction, I said I wanted you to tell yourself you're writing a novel from the first day, stating your intention as a way of building and maintaining drive and perseverance in the face of doubt and other negative emotions. It's also worth remembering that the task of any individual day is *never to write a novel*. A novel isn't usually drafted by your writing 60,000 to 100,000 words in one unbroken effort. More likely you'll write yours a couple hundred words per session, maybe a thousand or two thousand words on a great day.

In the generative novel-writing class I teach, I ask students to write 500 words a day, five days a week, for twelve weeks in a row, which adds up to 2,500 words per week and at least 30,000 words total by the end of the semester. It's an ask that always sounds daunting at the beginning of the course, but I've never had a student not reach the mark, especially because the goal is raw material, not polished, publishable words. You know what your life allows and what your process permits, but if you were able to commit to the same 500 words five times a week for a year, you'd have 130,000 words of raw material, easily enough for a novel or two.

I like daily goals, and I like the encouragement of this kind of simple math. For years, I had a goal of a thousand words every day I wrote; other years, it was two hours in the chair or "write from breakfast until lunch," however long that turned out to be on any given day. When I drafted my first-ever novel—a book I never tried to publish but that taught me I could write the necessary number of words—I did it in six months by writing five days a week, two hours each session, scheduled around my job as a restaurant manager.

These are ideals, but there are plenty of other ways to proceed. You'll also have to adapt to the changing needs of your life, with some weeks giving you more time to write than others. Sometimes my daily goal is only a single sentence, because that's all I can manage with my schedule, but I try never to go a day without looking at the book, which seems to keep my subconscious working on it. But that's me. Plenty of other writers have written good novels a paragraph at a time in the fifteen-minute gaps left by day jobs and child rearing or other responsibilities, while still others have drafted theirs in sprints at month-long writers' retreats.

While I believe it's good to set writing goals if you can (and crucial to forgive yourself when you miss them), you may also find you need to occasionally hide from the pressure you're feeling over the novel's outcome, whether that burden is self-imposed or put on you by the expectations of others.

How might you accomplish this hiding out, if and when you need it?

In an interview at *The Paris Review*, Garth Greenwell talked about how, while drafting the challenging middle of his novel *What Belongs to You*, he lowered the stakes by making the task more ephemeral: "I wrote it on scraps of paper, on receipts," Greenwell said. "It was like it had to be trash in order for me to write it. It had to be utterly dispos-able. I usually write in these spiral-bound school notebooks, which is a way of writing something that doesn't feel perma-nent, that doesn't feel important. But even that was too solid for the middle section."

This could be your situation as well. In order to proceed, you may have to pretend that what you're writing doesn't matter, that it's for you alone, that it's not that important: not chapters, but scenes; not scenes, but scraps of stray images. There's no right or wrong way to proceed. But do *proceed*. Even if you only rarely advance in a straight line, even if you do so most often by retreating and trying again, even if you go forward by steps so tiny you find it hard to believe you'll ever arrive at a full draft of your novel—as long as you keep writing, you'll make it.

One word at a time—it's all you have to do. It's more than enough.

Use a Working Title as a Target

Another trick you might use to convince yourself that what you're writing is already a novel is to attach a working title to your manuscript as soon as you can. I know it seems presump-tuous to name your book on the first day, but this working title (which you can always change) will serve a few functions as you proceed.

First and foremost, your working title might serve as a guide. Kevin Brockmeier once said, "I think of the title as the target toward which I shoot the arrow of the story," which I take as meaning that the title sitting at the top of my document can become a reminder of where I'm heading as I inch forward through my sentences. It's easy to get lost while writing a novel. A title might light the way ahead, in part by becoming suggestive of new material, additional thematic dimensions, or character traits, especially for your protagonist.

A good title, like a good sentence, often does double duty. It might have a literal meaning plus a subtextual or symbolic one. It might describe not only the protagonist but other characters in the novel as well. The title of Jesse Ball's recent novel, *Census*, for example, implies a task—the counting and cataloguing of the people of a country, identifying their unique traits, which is the central action undertaken by Ball's protagonist, a newly commissioned census taker—but it might also imply a more general taking stock, like the assessment of a life lived, which Ball's protagonist is also doing as he prepares for his own death and the orphaning of his autistic son.

The title of Jeff VanderMeer's *Annihilation* at first seems mostly thematic, referring to humanity's fear of destruction by the creeping disaster that is Area X—or else to the destruction of the natural world by human folly and greed—but the word *annihilation* also serves a plot function, appearing late in the novel as a crucial piece of weaponized language.

I don't suggest that you'll know all the meanings and uses of your title from the beginning of the process, but by having a title from the start, you might discover more of the possibilities that exist as you write. No working title, no chance at this kind of discovery—so, why not choose one? If you're trying to convince yourself you're writing a book, you're going to need to name your file *something* better than novel2.docx.

The other gift a working title provides is a proper name to refer to the book by, even if only in secret. Instead of thinking, *I'm writing a novel*, you can tell yourself, *I'm working on my novel*, the one titled *X*. Even when the manuscript is only a couple of thousand words long, the title makes it sound like something that already exists in full.

To name something well can be one way to love it. You will have to love your novel for a long time. So, give it a name you can love, as soon as you can.

Enjoy the Trappings of a Book

Another quick and easy way to make your on-screen document look like a book is to stick a cover page at the beginning. It's easy to do: put your newly chosen title in large font right in the middle of the page, hit Return, then type the word *by* followed by your name.

A Novel, by You, its writer—that's the end goal of this process. No reason not to claim it from day one.

Next, insert page numbers in the header or the footer, whichever you prefer. Put the title next to them, too. As you scroll through the document, this will subtly remind you of what it is you're making—the novel titled *X*—and also of the progress you've made in bringing it into the world, a manifestation that will be ever more tangible as those page numbers climb and climb.

Widen Your Page Margins

I learned this trick from Michael Kimball: experiment with how it feels to set your page margins to two inches instead of the standard one. This will reduce the amount of text on a single page, potentially making it easier to concentrate on what's there, and it will make the page on the screen look more booklike, which makes it easier to believe you're writing a book.

An added bonus: when you print off your manuscript, there'll be plenty of space in the margins for story ideas, additions of new text, and other notes to yourself.

Another benefit: tighter margins make the page count go up faster, which can create the illusion that you're making even more progress than you are.

Find Generative Epigraphs

While drafting, I often find lines in the other books I'm reading that could be potential epigraphs for the one I'm writing. Some of these speak directly to the thematic material I'm trying to address, while others serve as examples of the kind of prose I'm striving to write. Whenever I discover a bit of text like this, I stick it at the front of my manuscript (right after the cover page), so I see it first thing when I open the file. By the time I'm done, I often have five or ten or fifteen epigraphs, way more than can go in a finished book, but by then they've served their purpose, having reminded me of what I was trying to do with my novel when the draft itself couldn't tell me.

Track Your Progress

It can be hard to feel you're making headway, especially in the early going, so it's good to remind yourself of all the work you've done. For many years, I've kept spreadsheets to track first drafts, with columns for words written and hours written and formulas to total the two measures every day. If I write a thousand words in two hours, I write that down; if I skip a day, I put zeros in both columns.

I hate typing in those zeros, so this mild self-shaming is enough to make me write a little on days I don't think I can. Five minutes and fifty words is better than double zeroes. It's enough. Often, once I get those fifty words down, I find I can write another fifty, and so on.

In my spreadsheet, there's also a column where I jot some short notes, keeping a quick record of what went well, what I discovered that day, and what questions I might have for tomorrow. At the end of each month, I review my numbers and reread my notes, a recap that always makes me feel I've accomplished something, even if the recent writing has been a slog.

If you'd like a more tactile option, keep a physical log of your progress. While I was drafting my novel *Appleseed*, I for a time kept a Moleskine journal for tracking my writing process.

At the end of every writing session, I'd leave my office and go sit in the kitchen or the backyard and have a coffee or a drink while I recapped the day's work. I wrote a handwritten page or two every day, slowly thickening my journal with ink and use. That journal's physical transformation as I filled its pages made me feel I was accumulating something over time and offered the visceral sense of progress that a Word document or a spreadsheet doesn't necessarily provide.

YOU BEGIN

What's left now but to begin? Once you have some words on the page, you'll have something to work with, something to revise and rewrite and build upon. Until then, you don't! It's a scary moment, starting a novel, but there's no other way to begin than with one word, one sentence, one paragraph and page at a time. This might feel daunting, but it's impossible to avoid. Proceed bravely! As Sam Shepard said, "You have to take the plunge. It's easy to talk about the process, but it's a confrontation. You're confronting a blank page."

Getting started is always a challenge, but remember that whatever misgivings you might have about the earliest writing you do, it's better than the alternative, which is not to have written at all. Put the first words down, the first sentences, the first scenes, knowing that no matter how rough the writing is now, it'll eventually be improved through the rewriting and revision ahead. But you can't revise or rewrite or improve what hasn't been written.

WRITE TO PRODUCE INSPIRATION

So, you've started your novel: good work! I hope things have been proceeding well, but sooner or later, you'll run into the usual difficulties: your initial inspiration begins running low, you've got more happening than you can keep track of, you're alternating between days when the writing seems promising and others when you're embarrassed by it. Maybe worse than anything else, you're starting to stall, and you don't know how to regain your momentum. What next?

No matter how well things begin, eventually I get stuck, too, especially once I'm a good twenty or thirty thousand words into a draft. (So far, my experience has been that beginnings are easy, middles dreadful, and endings inevitable.) Whenever this happens, I take a deep breath and think of Lucy Corin's advice: "You should look at the material you produce to find your material . . . The story is always smarter than you—there will be patterns of theme, image, and idea that are much savvier and more complex than you could have come up with on your own . . . Become a student of your work in progress. Every aspect of a story has its own story."

Poet Traci Brimhall says she writes "in order to produce inspiration rather than at the mercy of it," and that's how I want to write, too, especially during this generative draft. When you get stuck, look at the material you've made and use it to produce fresh inspiration. It takes a lot of inspiration to write a novel. Here are some ways you might renew yours.

Writing the Islands

If you ever find yourself unsure of what comes next, try what Charlie Smith calls "writing the islands": instead of writing scene after scene in order (and *then* and *then* and *then*), write the big scenes you already know, no matter how far off they seem. Once those scenes exist on the page, the task then becomes writing between these known destinations, creating bridges to connect these islands.

The islands will need to be revised by the time you arrive at them again, once you know what else happens, but you're going to revise everything anyway. Don't let not knowing exactly what goes into a scene keep you from writing it.

A secret possibility: your exploratory draft might turn out to be nothing *but* these islands, discovered one after another; so might the final book. Contemporary novels usually need a lot less connective tissue than writers tend to assume. A classic example is the road trip novel, which could need only the stops, where some new trouble might happen, and less of the event-free driving in between. (Breakdowns are a likely story; smooth, trouble-free miles not so much—although, trapping two characters in conflict with each other inside a car for a long ride does have potential.) Better to write only the events, if you can, using the roadside attractions as your islands.

Follow Your Excitement

Writing the islands is also a way to ensure you're writing whatever you're presently most excited about, a good rule of thumb for drafting. Paying attention to your material and to your desire and enthusiasm in any given moment will spare you a lot of frustration. Writing the islands also means getting the best stuff you have so far out of your head and onto the page, making room for new best stuff to arise.

In general, if you're not excited about what you're writing, consider writing something else. But because I don't want you to abandon your novel in a fit of frustration, perhaps consider first writing *somewhere else* in the manuscript. Always go to where your energy is the highest. Your excitement will generate more excitement—and you will avoid the alternative, where your boredom generates more boredom.

Rachel Kushner says, "The writing has got to have this kind of energy where I think I'm onto something and I've figured out a track in the language to keep me onto that thing . . . I'm keen on a type of writing where I can feel the pleasure of the author." *The pleasure of the author* is one of the best guides that you, the author, can follow. Even before you know what your book will do for readers, you can pay attention to what it's doing for *you*.

Move toward pleasure, excitement, joy. Save nothing for

later. Spend your excitement and inspiration as soon as it appears, trusting that there's more where that came from. Put the good stuff down on the page as soon as it appears in your head and then use the good stuff that's there to imagine more good stuff.

Yes, And

Improv comedy, a collaborative form of real-time storytelling, is built around the idea of *yes, and*, which at its simplest means that when your fellow comedian asserts some new reality (*I'm a space janitor with a vertigo problem*), your job is to build on the idea by agreeing and then adding to it (*Yes, and the station's gravity keeps going on and off!*). As long as everyone onstage plays along, the communally improvised story builds in intensity and humor until it reaches its conclusion.

The alternative is to say no to your partner's suggestion. (*No, you're not. There's no such thing as a space janitor. That's dumb.*) But if you do that, then the sketch is over.

So, how can you put this tactic to work as a novelist?

By, again, being responsive to the material on the page.

Here's one way to think about it. Writing a novel isn't improv comedy, but cultivating a similar mindset to improv is useful. You write a sentence; it asserts a new reality, one that's surprising or strange, thrilling or off-putting. Then you read the sentence again, imagining the page is your improv partner, wanting to play, to create with you, if only you'll be agreeable to its suggestion.

So, you *yes, and* your sentence: you decide that the sentence you've written is true and then you build upon it, encouraging the story the sentence suggests. How can you heighten its effect or add to its reality?

When you're writing a novel, you and the page are alone in the room. But the material you've already made can be a great improv partner. This is one way the novel will suggest itself to you, growing from the good pages you've already made.

This is also a way of writing *recursively*, which at its simplest means to reach backward to find the material you need to move forward. Study the last sentence you wrote, the last paragraph or scene or chapter: What seems to have the most energy, the most heat, the most juice? Now take that element and try to carry it forward into a new sentence or paragraph or scene. When the new passage is as good as it can be, study it in the same way, looking for a good place from which to leap, push off, or otherwise depart.

One of the benefits of this method is that if each new sentence springs from some element of the one before it, there's a good chance the entire passage will end up feeling of a piece, as the material it's made of partly will be.

Read Predictively

As you study your material, be sure to read predictively: Based on your reading of scenes already written, what scenes do you predict might follow? What are the actions characters could take next to choose one outcome or another? Where are these characters headed, what do they want, and what will they do to get what they want? Can you see other foreshadowing or setups being put into place by the scenes already written? Is there groundwork being done for thematic issues, for the intellectual or emotional or moral questions your novel wants to ask?

Once you know these answers, write new scenes where the answers might live.

Predictive reading is a skill you can (and should) practice while reading other writers' published books. Pay attention to what threads are being set up in a novel's early chapters and then look to see how those threads are lengthened and where and when they pay off. How are your expectations fulfilled or subverted? After you've practiced this while reading other writers' published books, use this method to look for ways to extend the threads you're creating in your own work. Write scenes further troubling your earlier scenes and then move through those new complications toward reversal, climax, resolution. The chapters you've written so far are your best guides to the chapters you need to write next.

Beware of "Have To" Scenes

Watch out for any scene you feel you "have to" produce, especially if you don't want to write it. Don't flinch from necessary work, but also don't make scenes you're not interested in. Follow your intuition: if you find you lack the enthusiasm to write a particular scene you've planned, or even find it impossible to produce, maybe it's only that a different scene needs to go in the same place.

This feeling sometimes appears when you've borrowed the scene you're imagining from someone else's novel, or from a movie you've seen, or from the most well-worn tropes of the genre in which you're writing. When this happens, the problem is often that the scene is based on one whose beats fulfill the needs of its home story's narrative, not yours, and so those beats end up feeling false once imported into your plot. If you find this happening in your draft, put aside what occurs in the scene you're trying to write, its *content*, and consider its *function*: What function does your novel need its next scene to serve? How is it the same or different from the function of the scene that inspired you? If your scene's narrative function isn't the same as the one you're borrowing from, then anything inspired by it isn't going to work in the same way.

The other kind of "have to" scene that usually fails is one that's purely informational: you want to show how a character moves from place A to place B, or how they've acquired some necessary but ultimately minor object or knowledge. But often such scenes aren't interesting: we don't need to see the drive time between locales, unless you're filling that time with some other tension; and while gathering all the necessary and inventive gadgets can be a fun part of a heist narrative, I don't need to see your protagonist drive to Home Depot to buy the same tools I have hanging in my own garage, unless something unexpected is going to happen while she's at the store. Modern readers are savvy and smart, with a good idea of how stories work. You can skip the interstitial bits and move on to the next dynamic scene.

Learn What Book You're Not *Writing*

Several years ago, Alexis Smith visited a class of mine to talk about her novel *Marrow Island*. During the Q&A, she noted that she'd restarted the book several times over a period of years, putting aside failed openings until she discovered one that worked. According to Smith, what she wrote in those years didn't represent wasted time, because with every attempt, she learned more about what novel she *wasn't* writing, sorting through the possibilities of what her book might become by discarding what it shouldn't.

Working on my novel drafts, and reading those of my friends and students, I recognize this as an essential part of the process. You start writing one book, and as you write, you realize there's another, better book you could be writing, one you'll arrive at not by abandoning your draft but by changing your conception of it. In *The Triggering Town*, poet Richard Hugo explains that the subject that gets you started writing a poem is often only a starting place to work from until the poem reveals its truer subject. He writes, "Somehow you must switch your allegiance from the triggering subject to the words"—which is another way of saying that what your novel tells you it wants to be is ultimately more important than what you wanted it to be when you began.

Learning what your novel isn't will bring you closer to what the novel will be: when it stops telling you no, you'll finally be on your way.

FEED YOUR IMAGINATION

Imagination is not a static lump but, rather, a malleable (if mysterious) entity made of two primary substances: *art life* and *lived life*. As you write, you put these twinned substances to work together, and with them, you forge something wholly new. During your first draft, you'll need to draw upon the art/life experience you already have, while replenishing and enlarging your experiential stockpile whenever you find your supply of inspiration wearing down.

Art Life

Every novel I've written gradually accrued a project-specific foundation of other art: novels and short stories, poems and plays and essays, movies and music and visual art, all of which somehow felt in conversation with the book I was writing. Often this art foundation starts small, sometimes consisting of only a single example that serves as the model for the kind of book I'm writing. As time goes on, other art begins to stick to the project, to pile up, to suggest the larger conversation I'm entering. One bookshelf in my office is dedicated to the books supporting my current project; there are boxes in my closet filled with research materials from my published novels and for novels I haven't finished but apparently haven't fully abandoned.

Finding your art foundation will help you see how your book already has its fellows in the world, ancestors and companions to help guide you on your way. There's inspiration in this, and confidence and community and conversation. Some of my failed novels didn't work out because they never found their own invigorating community of books; maybe one day they will, and I'll be able to begin again.

Certain novelists say they don't read fiction while they're writing, for fear of being influenced. I personally *crave* influence—the more influences, the better. The writers I know who seem to be the most "original" or "innovative" often turn out to be the most diverse readers. It's not that they're without influence; it's that they're influenced by so many writers and styles and genres that it's difficult to separate any individual voice from the final synthesis. Crucially, this usually means not reading only current American contemporary fiction, and especially not only the kind of books frequently covered in *The New York Times* or *The New Yorker*. It means reading novels from big presses and small presses, conventional and experimental novels, novels of every genre, and novels in translation from all over the world.

The bigger you make your art life, the more possibilities your imagination will generate. I was a reader before I was a writer, and I would, if forced, choose reading over writing; I'm a writer because I was a reader who wanted there to be more books like the books I loved. Without a constant input of art, I stop wanting to make my own. I think that's a pretty common experience. So, keep yourself fed, keep your diet varied, keep putting enough art in so that art keeps flowing back out.

If you find yourself stuck while drafting, it's possible you've been reading too close to your project—that is, the books you're reading are so similar to yours that other possibilities aren't occurring to you. Switch up your intake: a change in genre will bring with it different tactics and craft techniques, additional solutions to narrative problems and alternative story structures. You want as many possibilities floating around you as possible, especially in the earliest and wildest stages of your draft.

Lived Life

The other source feeding your imagination is your lived life, the memories of your experiences up to this point and the emotions attached to those memories. Without doing any research, you bring a lot of this lived experience to the work. As Flannery O'Connor famously wrote, "Anybody who has survived his childhood has enough information about life to last him the rest of his days."

Assuming that you, too, have survived your childhood by the time you started your novel, what else might you still need to add to your lived life to write your book? And how can you best access those experiences as you write?

In my mid-thirties, I moved from Michigan to Arizona. For the first year that I lived in Phoenix, I struggled to write, and only months in did it occur to me why: nothing in Arizona made me think of home. Phoenix has seasons, but they're not as dramatic as Michigan's, and during my first year here, time seemed to fail to pass, with every day almost as sunny as any other. Plus, Phoenix, with its low, stucco sprawl, didn't remind me of the Michigan cities I'd known or the rural town where I'd grown up. I realized, too, that I hadn't even been dreaming; my imagination had shut down completely.

If my inability to access my memories had persisted, I'd have had to move home. But late that first year, I spent a week in Vermont, at a writers' residency, working in a cabin surrounded by pine forests, kept inside by a light summer rain. While I was there, my Michigan memories came flooding back to me: everywhere I went, there was some sight or smell or sound reminding me of *home*. That year made it clear to me that I'm a Midwestern writer and that I should lean into that rather than try to avoid it. Midwestern flora and fauna, Midwestern weather, Midwestern people with their emplaced patterns of speech and thought—no matter what I'm writing about, these are the things my mind reaches for first.

If I'm trying to write about a certain era of my life, I sometimes return to music or books or movies connected to the years or locations I want to remember. Other times, if the place itself isn't accessible, I look for analogues, somewhere new that reminds me of the place I've been. You may need to find your own local triggers, even if you're not doing autobiographical work, because so much of your natural imagery and your innate symbol system likely resides in this memory-rich part of your imagination.

You might also find you need to keep adding to your lived life as you write. You may decide to seek out certain experiences directly—Will Chancellor hiked across Iceland alone for eight weeks, mid–third draft, creating what he called "retroactive autobiography" for his novel, *A Brave Man Seven Storeys Tall*—but anything you do will create new connections and new insights. Eventually, as your novel grows in pages, you'll develop what I call a *form of attention* derived from the book: as you move through the life around you, you'll see it simultaneously with your own eyes and with the eyes of your novel. The book will notice different things from you, and so, the more places you take your form of attention, the more likely you are to find out what it's interested in, what it knows and wants to know about the world.

CREATING GENERATIVE CHARACTERS

Character Names and Physical Traits

I often feel tentative giving characters names for the first time: is this person a James or a Laurie, a Beloved or a Godslayer, a Veruca Salt or a Shasta Fay Hepworth? But over time, characters often come to fully inhabit the names I choose, until it's impossible to imagine their being called anything else. In this way, a good character name can be as generative as a good title—but the names of your characters are also chunks of language and sound you'll have to deal with throughout your book.

Whatever you call your protagonist, their name will become one of the most common words in your book, one of its most repeated sounds. One writer might like building sentences around Samwise Gamgee, but another might balk at having to constantly work with the same syllables. Think about the kinds of names that work best for your acoustics—or let your acoustics be shaped by a name's many repetitions, which will inevitably be at the heart of many of the sentences you'll have to write.

In addition, look for ways to ground the reader in your protagonist by using their notable physical traits: think of Ahab's whalebone leg, Gandalf's beard, Cindy Crawford's mole. The entirety of Ahab and Gandalf and Cindy Crawford can be brought to mind by simply mentioning their most prominent detail—and often these prominent details have their own back-stories and associations, so when we hear about Ahab's artificial leg, we are connected to a history of conflict. (All this is related to *metonyms* and *synecdoche*, but you don't have to remember the terminology to make the tactic work.) In the early going of the novel, such details can also suggest a fullness of character you haven't yet earned on the page.

Consider Captain Hook, a man whose entirety is contained

in every mention of his prosthetic. Or Little Red Riding Hood, a girl aglow beneath the slight scrawl of her bright red cape.

Keep Characters Acting

But what if you don't have a name at the outset? Then you'll have to find other ways to get to know your protagonist.

Writing the first pages of my novel *Scrapper*, I made a rule to keep my unnamed, unknown protagonist active: I could write any scene I wanted, in whatever order, as long as my protagonist was doing something that caused a change to occur, in him or in the world around him. I wrote scene after scene, moving him through the routines of his work until it revealed his inner life; I wrote down what he noticed, which taught me what he remembered and showed me what he feared. I discovered the entire plot of the novel by doing this: the central mystery of that book came out of exploratory writing, not out of planning and outlining.

This is one reason it's good for characters to have jobs. Who we are at work often isn't who we are at home, and how we feel about our occupation and how we complete its tasks reveal a lot about us. A dutiful and involved father who's also a lazy accountant feels differently about these two parts of his life, with home being more fulfilling than work. An assassin who dispatches her targets with calm competency seems like an old pro, while a deep-sea fisherman who gets seasick might be read as a newbie. Almost any task will do: an otherwise mild-mannered and withdrawn teenager who becomes volubly competitive during a game of Trivial Pursuit might be a *Jeop-ardy!* champion in the making another hundred pages down the line.

The Stories Characters Tell Themselves

Claire Vaye Watkins once said, "You need to know the story the characters are telling themselves, and then beyond that, you have to know the story your characters are telling themselves about the stories they tell themselves. We all have meta-narratives inside us." Elsewhere, Laura van den Berg told an interviewer, "I think both self-narrativizing and selective memory are essential survival skills," before quoting Joan Didion's famous line "We tell ourselves stories in order to live."

Both these writers were, I believe, paraphrasing Jim Shepard, who added (while being interviewed by van den Berg), "I'm really interested in how complicated our self-presentation can be: the way it can knit together self-indictment and self-exoneration so weirdly and completely. And the way in which that process is simultaneously unconscious and calculated."

These writers are all circling the fact that, ideally, many stories operate at once in a particular narrative: there is the story of the novel's present action, but also the stories your protagonists are telling themselves about their motives and their pasts. Crucially, there are also the stories one character might tell about another, stories they might or might not openly share with their subjects: There's the story a daughter tells about her mother's role in her childhood and the story the mother tells about the daughter as a child, and these two stories might be irreconcilable. And the difference might or might not be acknowledged between the two characters. A great misunderstanding might generate story and trouble, leading either to tragedy or to comedy, to the fracture of a family or to the healing of its rifts.

In some ways, we might all be living cases of mistaken identity, hiding or hidden behind masks or disguises or misapprehensions: Maybe our parents never gave up their idea of us as irresponsible teenagers, even after we'd proven ourselves capable of managing careers, marriages, families. Maybe we remember a now-sober acquaintance only by his regrettable past behaviors. The gap between the person a character is and the person they used to be (or are assumed to be) contains a lot of potential power.

As you progress, occasionally reread what you've written, looking for new trouble in the stories your characters tell one another or themselves. By coming to know your characters' stories, you come to know your characters. Let them show you who they are and how they came to be; pay attention to the places where they've done so already, and then write new scenes interrogating and testing the stories they tell, all in the hope of bringing them, through the action of the story, to some truer reveal.

Minor Characters: Reuse, Combine, Split Apart

It's common for me to continue to audition a variety of minor characters throughout the first draft, as I don't yet know who's who or what narrative functions characters outside the core cast might serve. Often a minor character appears because I need some object moved around a room, or a person to serve as a foil. But then I start liking that person—a funny bit of dialogue escapes their mouth, or they produce a reaction in my protagonist I didn't expect—and I become curious about where else they might appear. Can I reuse these minor characters in other scenes, letting the protagonist meet them again in different settings, or in the same place but under different circumstances? Minor characters don't need the same dramatic arcs as protagonists, so one way to produce contrast or to make change visible is to keep minor characters relatively static and then bring the protagonist into their presence again as the novel's situation shifts.

Other times, you populate the narrative with too many characters rather than too few. Say you decide your protagonist has three sons and then realize you've struggled to differentiate them. Maybe you've got an obedient son and a disobedient son and a son who is both obedient and disobedient. One solution to this overabundance of sons might be to combine two of them: one obedient son and one disobedient son are enough, and it's more dramatic without the agreeable flip-flopper taking up space.

If you're four hundred pages in when this happens, you've got a dilemma: Do you stop and fix the four hundred pages? Won't this kill your forward momentum?

It might. That's a lot of pages to correct. But because you're going to have to revise and rewrite later anyway, why not make the change in your head and continue on?

A grad student did this in the first novel-writing workshop I taught, gleefully holding the two alternate worlds of her novel in her head: one world in which a father and son coexisted, one in which the son took on both their former roles. When it came time to revise, she was already half-done fixing this particular problem, because in the second half of the novel, everything already worked the way it should.

Writing my novel *Appleseed*, I made the mistake of being more wishy-washy about a character's existence: I wrote a brother in, I took the brother out, I wrote him in, I took him out. I did exactly what my brave student did, but I didn't commit. Instead of making a choice and sticking with it, I had a character blinking in and out of existence. It was inefficient, confusing, frustrating—my novel had become haunted by my indecision. After a couple of cycles of writing scenes with and without the brother, I decided for the last time that he needed to stay. I knew I'd have to go back and fix a bunch of scenes where he was missing, but so what? I'd also have to fix the ones he was in, because in the end, I was going to have to fix *everything*. You can't wait until you're completely sure of some decision to move forward.

So often you learn what's right only by trying more than one solution in the same document, remembering always that efficiency isn't the goal; a great book is the goal. And the path to a great book is often winding and unclear, involving as much backtracking as it does clear progress. But there's nothing to do for it but to walk the crooked road you're on, believing all the while that it'll eventually lead you home.

REVIST YOUR SETTINGS

In your exploratory draft, consider reusing settings whenever you can. Your novel doesn't need a thousand locations—and can't have a thousand anyway, if you want to sell your movie rights someday. Rather than constantly inventing new locales, send your characters through the same settings again, whenever conditions have changed, which means whenever they have new knowledge, new problems, or new desires. See what those desires look like when the protagonist is brought back to the same spaces or is confronting the same characters again, characters who might also have changed in the interim.

I sometimes ask my undergrad students (who are usually only a couple of years out of their parents' houses) to tell me what it's like to go home again, to sleep in their childhood beds, to eat at their parents' table. Inevitably, my students tell stories about houses that have been sold, about former bedrooms that have become home gyms, about how small all the rooms in the house feel now. The house has or hasn't changed, but my students absolutely have. Even if their parents preserve their rooms as time capsules of their childhoods, arresting them at high school graduation, my students bring their own newness and change into these stale rooms each time they visit them.

Ridley Scott's *Blade Runner* is one of my favorite movies, and on a recent rewatch, I noticed how repetitive most of its staging it is. The film's set design gave us one of the most durable visions of the future in American pop culture, but all that imagined possibility was created with relatively few locations, mainly the Tyrell Corporation office, Deckard's apartment, J. F. Sebastian's loft, and the Chinatown streets and shops. Other settings appear once (for instance, the club where Zhora works), but well over half the movie takes place in the repeated settings. When Deckard returns to Tyrell, it's with new information and new suspicions; when Rachael leaves Tyrell and appears in Deckard's apartment, he finds her vulnerable and exposed, which changes the power balance between the two characters—but we also see Deckard's place through Rachael's eyes, watching her disapproving reaction to his disheveled bachelor pad.

If the number of locales in your novel has begun to feel ungainly, look through the settings you've already written and then write new scenes in the most promising ones. When your characters return to places they've already been, either they or the setting needs to have changed in the interim: A woman returns to her childhood home thirty years after she left, after having been a mother and a wife, finding the house disturbingly the same. Elsewhere, a young girl leaves home for school and comes back mere hours later to find the house ablaze, her burning possessions blowing in the wind.

Either way, something new will occur next. How could it not?

How does the woman, who has experienced so much, see the static home in new ways?

Who does the girl become after an otherwise normal day ends in tragic loss?

You change either the character or the setting, then recombine them again, so the element in motion can force its more kinetic energy on the element you've left at rest.

You cannot revisit your preserved childhood home as an adult without finding the rooms too small for the person you've become. You cannot enter your burning childhood home and escape unchanged.

DISCOVER THE RIGHT SCENES

One common discouragement early in a novel draft can be sensing a certain sameness to the prose or the shape of the scenes you're writing. This isn't necessarily a crisis, but it can leave you feeling flatter about the work than you'd like. Partly, this is because the opening of most novels—and this is truer of first drafts, when so much speculative, exploratory writing is happening—are spent establishing the status quo: What was the world of these characters like before the inciting incident?

Those kinds of scenes can feel a bit more static than later scenes, those you'll write once your characters become more active in their attempts to reach their goals.

There are many ways to overcome this creeping sense of sameness; one is to intentionally vary the outcomes of your earliest scenes. In Jeff VanderMeer's *Wonderbook*, he lists four elements by which we progress the plot: *discoveries, complications, reversals,* and *resolutions.* Most successful scenes in a novel offer the reader at least one of these elements. Discovery tends to be most prevalent early in a story, while the biggest reversal usually comes near the end, in catastrophic form, at the "all is lost" moment. But no matter where you are in the process, one way to progress when stalled is to set yourself a task to write four scenes: a discovery scene, a complication scene, a reversal scene, and a resolution scene.

The goal here isn't necessarily to get four perfect scenes, but to get moving again. At the very least, you'll come out of this with several thousand words, enough to jolt you out of whatever rut you've been in. If you're lucky, you'll have four dynamic scenes bringing you new information about your characters, fresh problems for them to overcome, and the suggestion of future events.

I've employed a similar tactic to good effect, taking inspiration from a *New Yorker* article about "scenario planning," in which Joshua Rothman reported that when organizations speculate on the outcomes of their actions, their "scenario-planning starter kit" aims to imagine three possible futures:

"You build one model where things get better, one where they get worse, and one where they get weird." If you're unsure what should happen next in your novel, you might get yourself unstuck by writing three scenes, either in sequence or as islands, aiming for these three outcomes.

Afterward, reflect on the different textures these scenes have and the different possible futures they suggest for your characters and your plot. Where might you go from here? What other scenes already written might benefit from this kind of additional permutation?

Turn Habitual Actions into Specific Action

In early drafts, I often find myself writing *generalized* or *habitual action*, scenes describing a character's daily routines or preexisting patterns of behavior. For instance, I might write, "Some days, Oliver couldn't bother to get out of bed." Or "When confronted by his mother, he would always come up with some excuse." And maybe "He was forever late for school, no matter what he or anyone else tried."

Some days, would, always, forever—these are indicators of ongoing, habitual actions, which is to say, actions that are most often not taking place in specific scenes, often predating the inciting incident of your novel. They happen before the changes the novel's story will bring about have begun. And while some excellent fiction makes heavy use of the habitual—*We the Animals* by Justin Torres, or the stories of Peter Markus, for example—in many novel drafts, the persistent presence of the habitual is an indication of an opportunity for generative revision.

Here you can use the savviness of readers to your advantage. We understand that any individual scene might be representative of other scenes, unseen: If we see a character being cruel in chapter one, we understand he's been cruel before. If we see a character fail to find the courage to leap off a high dive despite the urging of her peers, we'll know this happens all the time. So, instead of the habitual "Juliette would often balk at the end of the diving board," you might write, "Juliette told herself she could do it. She climbed the tall ladder, walked confidently to the end of the diving board, and prepared to jump. But as she looked down at the yawning gap of air above the flat, hard water of the pool, she began to doubt. From below, she heard the laughter of the other children, the same laughter as before."

The second version is richer in detail but still contains enough flags to tell us that this is Juliette's status quo. This is what might be changed by the events of the novel we're about to read: someday, if things go well, Juliette will become the kind of person who jumps off the diving board without hesitation.

The detail-rich version of this information may also be more likely to move the reader emotionally, because emotion is usually better delivered by scene than by exposition. By making more space for specific sensory information and in-the-moment interiority than summarized habitual action does, the scene better demonstrates Juliette's desire to be braver, and, because we're conditioned to cheer for the protagonist's wants, creates that same want in readers.

Expand a Single Act into a Series

Another way to generate more dynamic progress in your exploratory draft is to transform a single scene you've written into a series of scenes, returning to the same setting or repeating the same type of event multiple times. In the previous section, we met Juliette and her fear of high diving. A quick way to build the story would be to write the first scene, where Juliette balks and doesn't dive, which establishes the status quo of the story, and then to come back after a series of events has occurred (Juliette has set out to conquer her fears through increasingly outlandish bravery-building exercises), only to find out that despite Juliette's feeling that she's grown, she hasn't grown enough (Juliette, newly brave in so many other settings, still fails to dive). More events occur, Juliette is changed ever more powerfully, until we get a third scene on the high dive: this time, Juliette bravely jumps, much to the surprise of all the onlookers so used to laughing at her failure.

Another example: In the movie *Gattaca*, Ethan Hawke plays Vincent, an "in-valid" destined to a life of manual labor in a world where genetic selection produces a class of exceptional people who get the best jobs. Vincent's brother, Anton, is one of the "valids," and from a young age, Ethan is clearly no match for Anton physically, something we learn from a scene of the two brothers swimming out into the ocean depths, playing a game of chicken to see who will turn back first. As teenagers, Vincent flinches and turns back; another time, we see Anton save Vincent from drowning. At the movie's end—after adult Vincent has successfully impersonated a valid long enough to be selected as an astronaut—he and his brother swim one more time, going farther than ever before. This time, it's Vincent who wins their game, which ends with his saving Anton's life in an inversion of their last swim as teenagers.

The two scenes are essentially the same scene, repeated decades apart from each other. But conditions have changed, including who plays which part—winner and loser, drowner and rescuer—and so, the emotional resonance changes, too. What was once a demonstration of Vincent's inferiority becomes proof of his resilience and drive and his earned equality with his genetic "betters."

As readers, we find this kind of progression incredibly satisfying.

As writers, we discover its possibilities the same way we discover so much else: by looking back at what we've made in order to determine what we have yet to make.

Using Lists to Manage Time

A well-written list can create a heightened form of summarized exposition, used to move time along more quickly or to deliver larger amounts of information in compressed form. Even better, this heightened, fast-moving summary can be punctuated by *micro scenes* lasting only a sentence or two, breaking up the exposition by delivering bursts of precise detail.

In Lauren Groff's *Arcadia*, time leaps forward between eras at the end of each of the book's parts, forcing Groff to reground the reader in each new setting and to update the present state of the dozens of characters who inhabit the novel's commune where her protagonist, Bit, was raised. Here's how Groff reorients the reader to Bit's world when we rejoin him in young adulthood, several years after we last saw him:

After his very first episode of sadness, Bit returned to school and kept going until he graduated and went smoothly into college. His sophomore year at Cornell, when he was visiting Jincy at Smith, he heard that Helle had returned from Norway. Jincy was somehow the knot at the center of the net, the one who searched people out and stayed in touch with them. And over the years after the first sighting, it was Jincy who told him that Helle was modeling, mostly local stuff, JCPenney catalogs and ads. Then she'd gone out to Los Angeles. Then she'd gone to San Francisco. Then she was in rehab. Cole had become Bit's best friend again; they'd found each other at age twenty-four in a grocery store two blocks from where they both lived. Cole took over the narrative: Helle was married. The marriage was annulled. She was in Miami. Then, for a long time, nobody knew where she was.

Suddenly, Bit was thirty-five. Time, he often thinks, goes like that. He had grown tired of poverty, of scrambling for galleries' attention, the few solo shows not fulfilling enough, anymore. He had gone back to school for his MFA, had gotten an assistant professor position in the university.

Then one drizzly day in spring, Cole called Bit up, saying that Helle was coming to town . . .

Note how quickly we're moving through time: Bit goes from roughly high school age to thirty-five in the span of a few paragraphs. We're updated on a handful of characters along the way (Bit, Jincy, Helle, Cole), and then, when we meet Bit at twenty-four, time markers disappear along with every trace of Helle: "Helle was married. The marriage was annulled. She was in Miami. Then, for a long time, nobody knew where she was." In four simple sentences, eleven years pass: after the paragraph break, Bit's thirty-five.

In the next paragraph, we move out of this expositional listing of events and information and back into a scene with the inciting incident that kicks off the proper action of the novel's second part: Cole's call with news of Helle. Two decades have been covered in two paragraphs with enviable efficiency, returning us to the novel's proper action without confusion or delay.

It can be hard to know where in a first draft to put this kind of listed exposition (and its attendant micro scenes), but once

again, paying attention to the material you've already made
might suggest places to try it. Look for time jumps, as in *Arcadia*: usually you'll want to move from season to season or year
to year as quickly as possible, while also delivering the highlights of the skipped time. But anywhere you find yourself
plodding along, eager to get to the "exciting parts" of the
story, consider giving this technique a try: move through
the "boring" but necessary bits of your protagonist's life in
a list, alighting here and there on a detail or a mini-event, and
then use a specific and clear action to place the reader in the
next important scene, moving out of exposition and toward
detailed action and direct dialogue.

Counterpoint Scenes

In your exploratory draft, you might create generative opportunities by placing two disparate scenes or other story elements
in close proximity. As with pushing the two north-seeking
poles of a magnet together, this creates a kind of felt resistance,
which grows stronger as you try harder to make the two touch
or match up. Exploring this energy field of wrongness between
such counterpointed material may suggest new and interesting
and possibly stranger material you could write next.

You can create counterpoints and juxtapositions with images
and actions, with character traits, with tone, with topics and
ideas, with the gap between the expectations readers bring to
your settings and the language you use to describe those settings. In my early fiction, one of my favorite tricks was writing

about specific time periods with the "wrong" language, as in my novella *Cataclysm Baby*, in which I describe futuristic settings using purposely archaic syntax and diction. Writing a story about contemporary life in an invented, anachronistic vernacular remains more interesting to me than using the everyday language of, say, Twitter and television commercials. This tactic of mismatching subject and style often creates interesting aesthetic effects.

At some point in your first draft, you'll believe you know what material belongs and what either clearly doesn't or seems more difficult to fold in. One tactic to generate new ideas at this stage might be to write a scene in which both the most obvious thematic material of your draft and the most ill-fitting are melded. Or you might take two events that don't naturally go together and put them in the same space and time: a marriage proposal at a funeral, perhaps.

Think about tone: What happens when you put incongruous elements together? We all swim in so many discourses (academic, advertising, political, the languages of various subcultures), and using these discourses in a wrongheaded way can be surprisingly generative. This was one of David Foster Wallace's go-to tactics: *Brief Interviews with Hideous Men* is full of moments when characters employ philosophical or theoretical ideas poorly or to bad effect, as when two of the "hideous men" use their knowledge of the terminology of feminist theory to reach clearly misogynistic conclusions.

Sometimes the only way to find out if wildly different

themes or settings or genres can work together is to force the fit—not on your mind, but on the page. Put the two repelling pieces of your narrative magnet as close as you can to each other and then write what you see in the energy field they generate.

Time Narrated versus Time of Narration

Another scene-level choice to consider is when and where the story is being told. A ten-year-old telling a tale in real time is necessarily constrained by their limited experience and faculties. A hundred-year-old person looking back on the same events would bring a lifetime of experience and education to bear on the telling, with the added complications, perhaps, of unreliable or failing memory.

As you draft your novel, you'll have to make some decisions about *time narrated* versus *time of narration*, which could have a drastic effect on how your novel reads and what your options are as a storyteller. To put it as simply as possible, *time narrated* is the amount of time the action of your novels covers; *time of narration* is the moment in time from which the story is told. If our hypothetical ten-year-old's story takes place on Christmas Eve 1940—perhaps an encounter with someone the child believes is Santa Claus, but who is actually their estranged father in disguise—then that night is the time narrated. Our time of narration could be the same evening, it could be a month later, or it could be, in the case of our century-old reflective narrator, Christmas Eve 2030.

Each of these choices offers different options for reflection, exposition, and authority, so consider testing different times of narration to see what possibilities exist for your story. Remember that you can establish patterns of point of view, flipping between times of narration, or you can use a time of narration shift only once, as a surprising interruption or correction. In the example just given, you could narrate from the ten-year-old's perspective for the bulk of the story while reserving the option to switch to the hundred-year-old's take at any time, in separate chapters or in momentary bursts of a few sentences—or you might do so only once, in a moment so surprising it recasts everything the reader has experienced so far.

Read a scene or chapter that isn't quite working, analyzing time narrated and time of narration as you read. Then try changing the time of narration, either by rewriting what you have or by adding to it. Later, you write on top of the ten-year-old's in-the-moment narration, "I would know there was no Santa Claus. I was fooled only in the moment. It was only then that I believed, but that belief, which I no longer share, made what happened between my father and me possible."

Steer Toward the Rapids

As fiction writers, we create compelling characters, we fall in love with them, we put them in terrible situations we wouldn't wish on anyone we know—and then we figure out how these invented people we've come to love might save themselves from the trouble we've put them in. It's tempting to give them an easy way out, especially if the conflict you've invented is uncomfortable or complicated, but whenever you can, avoid providing your characters a simple exit from their problems. Anywhere you find you've made your characters' lives too easy, revise the scene to make life harder.

As George Saunders says, the job of the writer is to "move toward the complicated" or to "steer toward the rapids," not away: in other words, move your characters into trouble, not out of it, as often as possible. Most stories are about tension and conflict, physical danger or emotional complexities; the goal is usually more obstacles, not fewer. Keep adding problems to scenes already written and then send your protagonist to solve the new problems. Something interesting will happen—and if it doesn't, then add another problem and try again.

I often find that I have several sources of tension spread throughout my first draft, all of them operating discretely, inside their own scenes. As I revise, I might move multiple tensions together into a single scene: It's one thing to have told a lie to a loved one, but what happens when a second loved one, whom you've told a contradictory lie, joins the conversation? And then a third person, and a fourth?

It's not enough to put your protagonist between a rock and a hard place. You want many rocks, many hard places.

What happens next will be trouble, and trouble is story.

The Obligatory Scenes of Genres

What is the genre of the story you're telling, and what can knowing this tell you about the scenes that must be included in your novel to meet the genre's expectations?

Maybe, at heart, your novel is a crime drama, or a romantic comedy, or a tale of extraplanetary colonization—even if you're writing a contemporary realist novel about "how we live now," likely its plot hews to some existing shape. That's why there are so many literary fiction retellings of *King Lear* or *Macbeth*: Shakespeare is a genre that literary fiction writers tell themselves is suitably highbrow but that still gives them a skeleton they can hang their material on.

Whatever genre your story most resembles likely suggests a few obligatory scenes. If you're writing a murder mystery, you need (at minimum) a scene where a body is discovered, a scene in which the detective accuses the criminal or otherwise explains the solution to the mystery, and a resolution in which justice is either served or thwarted. If you don't have those three things hinted at (or, more likely, directly depicted in a scene), it's not a murder mystery.

Once you know the primary genre of your novel, list the obligatory scenes that this kind of story usually contains, in your experience. Which ones are missing from your novel? Go write them! This is a good way to generate new material and an *especially* good way to generate *story*, because most obligatory scenes advance plot.

Note that you can use these obligatory scenes as ways to

scaffold other kinds of stories, creating interesting innovations. The television show *House* resembles a police procedural set in a hospital: each week's mystery disease is the criminal, the sick patient the crime scene, and each episode presents a series of clues and red herrings to be discovered by a team of doctors serving as beat cops or minor detectives before the brilliant Dr. House reveals the true culprit, diagnosing the patient and solving the mystery with Sherlockian flair.

While you can't leave out all the obligatory scenes of a genre and still end up writing inside it, you can subvert a reader's expectations by carefully omitting one or by putting something unexpected in its place. The 1959 movie *Anatomy of a Murder* in many ways follows the conventions of other court-room dramas, but it leaves out two expected scenes, to great effect: we're never shown the crime itself, even in flashback, which prevents us from forming an objective understanding of the event separate from what the unreliable characters tell us happened; and there are no closing arguments, leaving us to imagine how our lawyer protagonist wins the day.

The lack of the closing argument scene is especially nota-ble in *Anatomy of a Murder* because it's unclear whether the lawyer, played by James Stewart, is doing the right thing: Is he defending an innocent man or freeing a guilty one? A clos-ing argument in which he compellingly takes the moral high ground might skew our view; without it, a gap in the film's logic is created for the viewer to fill in on their own.

Inside this gap lies ambiguity, and it makes the ending of

Anatomy of a Murder more unsettling than it otherwise would have been, without affecting the resolution required by the genre, as the court case still ends in the obligatory scene of the verdict delivered and the criminal either punished or set free.

Set (or Reset) the Clock

One reason some early drafts feel baggy is that they're taking place over too large a span of time, or else the span of time they cover simply isn't defined yet. Once you've got some idea of what your novel's plot is, can you determine the smallest span of time the book's present action needs in order to unfold successfully?

A novel taking place over three days is likely tighter than the exact same story spread over thirty years, and there's inherent drama in letting your readers know the novel is of a fixed length. Chris Bachelder's *The Throwback Special* isn't a plot-driven novel, but at its onset, it lets the reader know a particular event is guaranteed to occur in three days. An ensemble cast of twenty-two characters has gathered at a hotel for a weekend to reenact a particular football play, a ritual these friends celebrate every year. When the friends arrive at the hotel, the novel starts; when the football play begins, the novel ends. Every other event in *The Throwback Special* exists in the promised three days between these points. It's enough! The ticking clock of *any* moment at which a novel is guaranteed to arrive will create tension and suspense and a reason to keep reading.

In *The Curtain*, Milan Kundera writes of what he calls "the beauty of a sudden density of life," a "rapid series of encounters . . . like three long notes played each on a different instrument and bound together in a single chord." The shorter the clock, the more likely you are to create this effect, compressing your story until events overlap, bump against one another, creating frictions and fissions and previously unforeseen opportunities for trouble and conflict and story. (There are extreme examples of very short clocks stretched to novel length, as in Nicholson Baker's *The Mezzanine*, which is crammed into a single escalator ride; narratives this short often take place mostly inside the protagonist's mind, as stream of consciousness.)

A related question: Is there some fitting background event that, while short in actual duration, feels like a longer span of time, possibly allowing you to compress your novel's action by setting it during that event? A novel taking place over Fourth of July weekend is technically contained in a shorter span than one spread over an entire summer, but can't a holiday weekend, with its gatherings of friends and family, with fireworks displays and local festivals, with too much to eat and drink, with unwanted sunburns and unshakeable hangovers, be made to feel like a whole summer's worth of activity?

Note also that because you have access to memory and flashbacks and other tools for bringing the past into the present action of a story, confining a novel's present events to a short time frame doesn't mean limiting your temporal scope. James Joyce's *Ulysses* and Virginia Woolf's *Mrs. Dalloway* unfold over a single day, but through the use of interiority and flashback, they both include much that occurred in the personal or historical pasts of their characters and settings.

A related way to discover the clock of your novel might be to identify a possible backdrop historical event, some kind of approaching drama that the reader might know about even if the novel's characters don't. For instance, Jesmyn Ward's novel *Salvage the Bones* takes place in the twelve days leading up to Hurricane Katrina, confining the novel's family drama to a short period while ensuring the reader knows what massive tragedy awaits at the novel's end, with disaster looming ever closer as the pages turn.

GETTING UNSTUCK: INTERRUPTIONS AND PLAY

One trap you might fall into early in a draft is becoming too sure of what your novel is, what its precise rules are, and where its limits lie. When I find myself stuck in this way, I often shake myself out of my rut by reaching for my grab bag of exercises, including those I've written for my students. Then I try to complete the exercises within the project I'm working on: What might this assignment produce inside the world of my novel?

If you don't already have your own favorite exercises, let me suggest a pair of books by Brian Kiteley, *The 3 A.M. Epiphany* and *The 4 A.M. Breakthrough*. They're filled with tricky assignments (some of which may be technically impossible) sure to get your brain moving in new ways. You might also check out the newsletter I write, at mattbell.substack.com, where you'll find monthly craft essays and writing exercises, many of which are based on activities I invented to shake up my own novel-writing process.

Wherever you get your exercises, the constraints of the assignments will ideally push you out of your rut and into new modes of thought, exposing previously unseen possibilities for the narrative voice, for your characters, for the kinds of scenes you might write.

New Points of View

If you find yourself stuck or bored or unable to figure out what to do next, experiment with a single scene that isn't working as well as you'd like by rewriting it from another point of view. Even if you change it back later, it might help you see the work anew. I often rewrite problematic first-person narratives into third and then back again, because my third-person voice allows for a lot less interiority than my first-person voice does, and so tends to get my character out of their head (or me out of theirs) and back to acting again.

Andrew Ervin once said that he writes every first draft in first person, then revises into third person, presumably to similar effect. This level of point-of-view change might be too extreme for you, but the urge makes sense: at some point in every novel, I've become convinced that my first-person narrator would be better in third person, or vice versa. Working on my novel *In the House upon the Dirt Between the Lake and the Woods*, I translated one hundred pages of the second draft from first to third person and then decided I had been right to tell the book in first person after all—but because I'd edited other elements with the changed POV, to keep those gains, I had to rewrite them again as I reverted back to first person. It took a long time, but afterward, I was sure of the point of view I'd chosen—and I'd done two rounds of heavy revision while figuring it out.

As you rewrite, consider whether any of the points of view you've tried creates additional opportunities at the language level for thematic or emotional effects. For instance, in the novel just mentioned, the protagonist, an unnamed husband who never calls his spouse by name, says the words *my wife* repeatedly, reinforcing his obsessive and toxic possessiveness, an effect that would be lost in the third person, when his spouse would become *the wife*, assuming she didn't start going by her name. If I hadn't gone through my long point-of-view translation, I might not have discovered this unexpected outcome in time to strengthen its effect.

In your novel draft, some nuance might likewise emerge from a new point of view that will end up reinforcing the book's ideas or themes or your character's emotional journey. If you see such an opportunity, move toward the richer point of view, then work to extract as much possibility as you can from the complexities it offers. These possibilities won't be the same for every novel, because no two first-person narrations are alike—no more than any two people are alike.

Remember, too, that many of the complications mentioned earlier (such as the gap between the time narrated and the time of narration) will continue to alter how any given point of view functions: there may be more than one kind of third-person narrator operating inside your novel, even if they're two versions of the same person, speaking from different points in time.

Change Up Your Storytelling Modes

Many conventional contemporary novels start in one mode—most often a third-person limited point of view written in the past tense, progressing by scenes presented in chronological order, broken up by occasional flashbacks—and then end in the same way. But that's not the only option available, either in kind or in duration: there's no rule that says you have to finish as you began.

Consider Claire Vaye Watkins's novel *Gold Fame Citrus*. It opens in a retrospective third-person limited, following Luz Dunn as she struggles to subsist in a dystopian Los Angeles, where she and her boyfriend, Ray, eventually rescue/abduct a mysterious child named Ig. The story continues in third-person limited for the first section of the novel, before Watkins breaks into other modes, including a history of the sand dune sea that's swallowed most of the American West, a character's psychological evaluation test, and an illustrated bestiary of the new wildlife that's emerged since the disaster began. Most of these alternative modes appear only once; they're rarely referred to by the novel's characters, and in some ways, they aren't "essential" for a mere recounting of the book's plot (which isn't to say they don't do work or don't belong in the novel).

What I believe—and Watkins said something to this effect to my students—is that regardless of what these mode switches provide for the *reading* of the novel, they were essential to its *writing*. Watkins worked in one mode (the conventional third-person limited of so many novels) until she stalled out or needed to create a change in texture or simply wanted to play around with what else the novel might do. She switched into another mode, plying it until it was played out, and then switched again.

I'm speculating here—I'm imagining a mode of thought useful to me, rather than trying to accurately depict Watkins's—but perhaps you see how much fun this mode switching could be, as a way of making progress. Your book doesn't have to be one continuous scroll of the same mode of storytelling. If what you're doing stops working, don't give up before you've tried proceeding in a new way.

A detective novel could switch from narration to police notes or evidence write-ups or forensic reports. A monster thriller could delve into the mind of the creature instead of its hunters. Certainly, a fantasy novel can take a break for a map or a legend or a song.

Whatever keeps you writing. That's the number one rule of the first draft.

The Circle of the Novel

In her essay "The Circle of the Novel," Jane Smiley talks about twelve kinds of discourse the novel might contain: *travel, history, biography, the tale, the joke, gossip, diaries and letters, confessions, polemics, essays, the epic,* and *romance.* Smiley argues that while almost every novel includes the biographical—"the sense that the reader comes to understand a character completely, better than the character understands himself or herself"— most great novels make use of a number of these forms at once.

Look at the material you've produced so far: Which of Smiley's discourses do you see already in play? Which could be added to introduce new kinds of narrative and textual variety? Write local legends between chapters. Think about the structures of jokes. Compose letters or emails from your characters. Consider the historical and social constructs your characters live inside and how those might drive or complicate what's on the page. If your book contains a travel narrative, it might be interesting to think what essayistic questions your character's trip could ask along the way. Test out what might fit and look for ways to create new generative energy to keep yourself writing. Think especially about what you've been trying to put into your novel that you haven't been able to make work so far. Could using a different discourse be the way to bring that material in?

As useful as these ideas are, my favorite part of Smiley's essay—and one of my favorite quotes about novel writing, period—comes at the end: "Greatness in a novel does not depend upon perfection of the object; perfection of the object is merely an added dimension to the greatness of certain novels. But every great novel offers incomprehensible abundance in some form."

Whatever else you do, keep finding ways to add more "incomprehensible abundance" to the splendor and possibility already present in your draft. This quality will one day thrill your readers, but it will also sustain you in the work. If all goes well, you will feel the novel expanding not only in page length but in possibility and wonder, the potential of the world you're making growing larger with every word you write.

Conduct Generative Research

One way to use the material you've made to get unstuck is to take time to research everything that appears in the story so far: the architecture of your setting, the models of cars people drive, the flora and fauna populating the landscape, the specific meals characters eat and drink, and so on. Check the reference books on your shelf. Google everything you can. Follow the bottomless rabbit holes of Wikipedia links, each link leading you deeper into your subject. You'll find a couple of inaccuracies to correct in your text, but that's the minor gain. The hope is that this kind of research will lead you to killer details you can use to punch up your story and that new ideas will occur to you as you discover areas of interest you didn't know your book had.

My personal rule about novel research: I never take notes

separate from my main manuscript, especially once I've started writing. If I find a fact or a detail I want to include, I don't write it down anywhere unless I can write it directly into the novel, either by finding an existing scene where it can live or by starting a new one centered on the fact or detail. That way, I don't generate a separate document full of inert, nonnovelistic prose, which feels so different from the kind of language I want my novel to contain. This practice has the side benefit of letting my research tell me what to write next: your research questions will guide you as powerfully as any whisperings of plot can, especially if you do your note-taking inside your novel, in the voice of the book.

In addition to the kind of research you do online or at the library, consider visiting the real-life places you're writing about, if you have the means and the opportunity; so many sensory details can be learned only when you're standing in a place. The instinct of many novelists is to do their travel research early in the process, but consider waiting to go until after you've written all or most of a draft. Earlier, I mentioned how each novel creates its own form of attention; you'll benefit so much from taking your novel's unique way of seeing to the closest match you can get to its setting, especially later in the process, when this form of attention is strongest.

Visiting the buildings or landscapes or communities where you've set a story feels different from visiting places you might write about: often a strange déjà vu or doubling of experience occurs when standing in a room you've been living in imaginatively for a year. While writing my novel *Scrapper*, I decided it would begin and end in the ruins of the abandoned Packard plant in Detroit, a building I'd seen from the highway but had never visited. I began the book while living in the Upper Peninsula of Michigan, eight hours away, so most of my research on the plant's interior happened through newspaper articles, the shaky YouTube videos of urban spelunkers, and other secondhand sources. But during the second draft, I went back to Detroit and visited the site with a local photographer, who showed me a lot of features I couldn't have seen online; and then I walked into the dangerously crumbling structure on my own, going only far enough to stop smelling the outside air, wanting to get a taste for the trapped feeling I'd decided my protagonist had felt in the scenes I'd already written.

That experience, along with others I had in Detroit after having written a draft, changed the novel for the better—not necessarily at the level of plot, but certainly at the level of detail and texture. The last scene I wrote for that novel was a thematic cornerstone I wouldn't have rendered as I did if I'd visited the building where it was set too early, before I knew what my protagonist would notice there, armed with all the emotions and memories and wants he'd carry into the space. I needed to have most of the novel written before I took the trip, so I could know what the novel wanted to see.

Finally, as I revise, I often move my nouns (and my descriptive metaphors and similes) ever closer to the concrete, seeking to learn proper nomenclatures, all the specific killer details that one of Virginia Woolf's characters names "the divine specific." In Don DeLillo's *Underworld*, a priest teaches a boy the names of all the parts of a shoe, saying that "everyday things represent the most overlooked knowledge," before ending his lesson with a riff on the word *quotidian*, a "gorgeous Latinate word . . . that suggests the depth and reach of the commonplace."

The depth and reach of the commonplace. Using the right names for objects and actions adds a felt substance to the page, while too many metaphors or similes can make a story seem abstract or removed: if everything is *like* something, then nothing *is* anything. Mine the vocabularies of your characters' occupations, each of which has its own special language. Learn the proper names of the plants and animals populating your story, the way locals refer to the locations and infrastructures of the cities and towns in which your novel is set. This is verisimilitude at the level of the sentence.

As the narrator of Clarice Lispector's *The Hour of the Star* says, "When I write—let things be known by their real names."

Embrace the Quiet/Loud Dynamic

One of the most consistently enjoyable shifts a rock song can make, for me, is when a quiet song suddenly becomes a loud one, or a loud one turns quiet, or when a fast part gives way to a slow part, until it gets fast again, and so on. (The Pixies are frequently cited as pioneering what would become the particular loud-quiet-loud pattern that I came of age with, influencing Nirvana, Radiohead, and countless other bands to write similarly structured songs.) In prose, the variations you create in sentence length, paragraph size, and scene duration produce much of the pleasure of reading and are in large part your "instrument" begging to be played well. As Ursula K. Le Guin said, "There is no optimum sentence length. The optimum is variety. The length of a sentence in good prose is established by contrast and interplay with the sentences around it—and by what it says and does."

Take a look back at what you've written and think a bit about the size of your primary units of sense: the sentence, the paragraph, the scene, and the chapter. Perhaps you naturally vary these as you go, but for most of us, a "default" move tends to rule our first drafts, perhaps the twelve-clause sentence, the two-page scene, or the page-buster paragraph. Maybe even the three-unit list of examples, a preference you'd be sharing with this writer.

Once you've identified your "default speed," do something to disrupt it. If you've been writing half-page scenes, write a five-pager. If you've been writing five-page scenes, see what your novel does with the fragment. Write a page-long sentence and kick out of it with a sentence of five or ten words long.

Go and go and go, as long as you can.

Then stop.

Michael Martone says, "A story is always a controlled crash. Not the line but the blot." I like the idea of a controlled-crash paragraph: a long, out-of-control sentence, one with an unreasonable number of clauses, the language continuing to rush forward, looking for what lies behind every trapdoor and cul-de-sac and side alley the syntax might offer, unearthing parentheticals inside em-dashed phrases, reinvigorating itself with a canny use of italics—followed by what?

The blot.

Go to it! Write short, write long, write differently from how you've written so far.

Vary Tone and Texture

Search for places where you might profitably vary the tone of the novel. In so many novels, a humorous moment comes right before crushing tragedy or a devastatingly emotional reveal. Why is this such a common move? In part, because unbroken progressions of the same kind of emotion don't *progress*. To feel as fully as we might, we need pauses and breaks, changes in tone and texture; we enjoy being moved through a spectrum of emotion. A joke sets us at ease, makes us feel comfortable; an unbearable tragedy demands eventual relief.

If you look at your outline and you see catastrophe after catastrophe with no breaks, some other element might be needed to break these moments up, whether it's a calmer or quieter moment, a humorous interlude, or a formal break into another storyline or mode of discourse. By skillfully and consistently creating these variations, you offer your readers another kind of suspense, ensuring that the next scene's effect will hit all the harder for the variety you've introduced.

The Argument and Other Adornments

One of my favorite literary devices is the *argument*, the brief summaries that appear in some novels at the beginning of each chapter, between the title and the text. The first place I saw them was likely in fantasy novels I read as a teenager, but the example that comes to mind now is from Cormac McCarthy's *Blood Meridian*. Here's the argument from that novel's first chapter:

Childhood in Tennessee—Runs away—New Orleans—Fights—Is shot—To Galveston—Nacogdoches— The Reverend Green—Judge Holden—An affray— Toadvine—Burning of the hotel—Escape.

As you might expect, this is more or less an outline of what happens in that chapter, stripped to its bare essentials. Arguments aren't common in contemporary novels, but you can still use them as generative tools. If you're stuck and aren't sure what comes next, why not try lining up all the little inklings of future plot into an argument and then write it out? You could do this for the rest of the book, obviously: write arguments for chapters not yet written and then write the chapters. I do this as a way of putting to work all the loose odds and ends floating around in my brain at some midpoint of the draft: a partial action, a character I don't know how to use, a setting I've imagined but can't get my characters to visit.

If I break down McCarthy's argument, it looks something like this:

Backstory—Event—Setting change—Event—
Event—Setting change—Setting change—Character
introduction—Character introduction—Event—Character
introduction—Event—Event.

Whether you've read *Blood Meridian* or not, it's possible to see how this is a recipe for a dynamic and interesting novel opening: six events, three settings, three new characters, a smidge of backstory. That's enough! Assigning yourself those same kinds of scenes in any order might work to get you writing again.

Either write an argument from scratch or write one for scenes already drafted, analyzing them as I did McCarthy's, using whatever labels make sense to you. Doing so might show you places where something's missing or where there's too much of one kind of scene in a row.

You're likely drawn to other parts of book layouts: some writers love chapter titles, some put epigraphs everywhere (I remember Dean Koontz having a particular fondness for the chapter-opening epigraph), some love the interruption of an illustration, hand-drawn or otherwise, as in Edward Carey's *The Swallowed Man.* Think about the favorite physical or textual elements of books you love and then add those elements to your novel as prompts for further writing.

It's a good rule of thumb: adding anything you love to your manuscript is a way to make you love it more, and any manuscript you love is something you'll want to spend more time working on.

GENERAL REVISION TACTICS FOR THE FIRST DRAFT (AND BEYOND)

One Thing to Fix in the Morning

One way to fold revision into a daily writing practice is to skim your manuscript right before bed, looking for one concrete thing you can fix first the next time you return to it. It can be any error you see, no matter how small: a typo, a line you'd like to improve, a paragraph that needs a trim. When you return to the desk, start your writing session by fixing the problem you found the night before. That way, even before you start composing new material, you'll know you've already improved the novel today.

I do my nightly check-in by looking at the manuscript on my e-reader, where I can highlight or annotate but not edit, a useful kindness at the end of the day. The novel looks so different on my device that I often feel more affectionate toward it there than when seeing it in Word. Word is the place where I struggle, while my e-reader is a place where I read published books. It's another small but welcome confidence trick.

So much of novel writing is about refreshing your confidence wherever and however you can. The entire enterprise is a long passage through uncertainty, and you're going to need every boost you can find.

Every Day, Retreat Three Pages (but, Sometimes, Retreat Thirty)

Almost every day, I rewind from where I last left off and revise a few pages. It's a way to settle into the desk, but it also helps me get the voice flowing again and, more often than not, gives me something new to write today. As William H. Gass said, "What I have written must tell me what to write next. If it does not, it must be rewritten until it does." While I'm revising, when I'm paying attention to what I've made, my brain is always trying to figure out what's coming next.

Some days, this doesn't work. Some *weeks*, this doesn't work. Whenever I truly don't know how to go on, I back up thirty pages and revise forward again, trying to improve what I can and gathering imaginative momentum so I can hit the edge of the manuscript running. More often than not, this helps. But sometimes, I have to do it again; sometimes, you will, too. If you don't know what to write next, make what you've already written better, more itself, more you. Staying at the desk while you do this—working even while you're lost—will mean you're already at the keys when inspiration returns. And sooner or later, it will, if you keep at it.

Remove the Boring Bits

At some point, you'll have amassed thirty or forty or eighty thousand words, but no matter how much you've written, you know you don't have a *novel* yet. Don't panic! As the pages pile up, it can occasionally be a good idea to clean up the mess, getting rid of material you wrote to get to this stage but that isn't going to remain in the final novel. You may already know which passages those are, so go ahead and take those out, as there's no reason to keep scrolling past stuff you're not going to use.

If you'd like to push on this a little harder, you could also read through the novel as it is, making a marginal note anywhere you (reading simultaneously as writer and reader) feel bored by what's happening. After you've marked all the boring parts, go back into the story and delete them all. Then read the draft again.

With luck, you might find that once you've removed all the "bad" bits, the rest of the draft seems cleaner and clearer, making the real trajectory of your novel more evident. But chances are, you'll need to put something in some of those gaps, possibly some version of what you've cut. But *write it from scratch*.

Start fresh. Don't tie yourself to boring events, actions, or sentences. It's usually easier to make a new scene from scratch than to make a bad scene good—but as I've just advised, if you can find one good thing to salvage out of each "boring" passage, try using it to start your new version.

A Note on Throwing Away Words

The first rule of throwing away words is *don't throw away words*. Instead, establish a "cut" file in the same directory as your novel and put anything you cut in there. Don't worry about keeping it organized or doing anything other than copying and pasting there anything you're about to throw away, instead of deleting it. Do this, and you'll become braver about making cuts, because you can always put the material back. You may find a place later where the cut passage might work again: often a sentence or idea that fails in one place works great in another. Some writers also manage to make all kinds of new stories and scenes out of their junk pile. I'm mostly not one of those writers, but you might be.

Just in case, keep everything.

A related tactic is to write (or edit) with Track Changes on. Seeing everything I've added for a day in red makes the work I've done visible, offering a sense of a job well done. It also makes me feel free to cut my prose up, to delete some chunks and move others, because it's so easy to undo the changes. I almost never reverse my choices, but knowing I can is freeing enough.

The One Good Thing

An even more extreme but often effective revision tactic: take a page of your most lifeless or stuck prose, scan it one more time to pick out the best sentences, and then retype those sentences onto a new page.

Next, move everything else on the bad page into your cut file.

Now go back to your salvaged and retyped best sentences and begin again.

Sometimes a great sentence gets swallowed by a pile of weaker prose or unworkable ideas or a stalled scene. Rescue it and try again. You'll be surprised at how much life there can be in a good sentence, once you've set it free. Start from your one good thing, then carry its goodness forward into new prose for as long as you can.

The Christine Schutt Challenge

If it seems I've been avoiding talking about sentence-level craft up to this point, there's a good reason for this: I don't want you to worry about it too much right now. But if you ever want to pause amid the generative chaos and the occasional slapdashery of this exploratory draft for a concentrated attempt to write the absolute best sentences you can, you might take what I call the Christine Schutt Challenge, described here in Schutt's own words: "Composition of one unimpeachable sentence in work of any length should be considered a victory."

You could do that a couple thousand times in a row and be done.

But, probably, you'd still have to rewrite. So, don't sweat it. Write the best prose you can, all in service of later writing prose that's even better.

FINISHING THE FIRST DRAFT (WHILE NOT WORRYING ABOUT YOUR SENTENCES)

I hope all these tips and tricks and habits and games will help you make your way through the daunting task of writing your first draft. For me, it's the most difficult phase of novel writing. Filling a blank notebook or a blank document with tens of thousands of words never gets any easier, and the uncertainty involved in doing so always presses down on me. Deborah Eisenberg once described the process like this: "You write something and there's no reality to it. You can't inject it with any kind of reality. You have to be patient and keep going, and then, one day, you can feel something signaling to you from the innermost recesses. Like a little person trapped under the rubble of an earthquake. And very, very, very slowly you find your way toward the little bit of living impulse."

All these tactics we've been discussing are ways you might reach the living impulse of your novel. Doing this requires rigorous self-kindness, a mindset as free of comparison with others or harsh judgment as possible. You want inventiveness, play, imagination; you may not receive polish or perfection at the same time. The first draft of your novel will likely not look like a book you pick up off the shelf of a store or a library, and why should it? Published novels have little to teach you about how books are written; they tell us only what novels can do once fixed in their final form.

Anne Lamott famously suggests writing "shitty first drafts," a concept many of my students cling to for comfort while simultaneously not believing in it. They want their first drafts to emerge already perfect, even though experience and advice tell them this is not possible. That said, you *will* write some beautiful sentences during your first draft, and those sentences will give you the strength to keep going. Often, in my own drafts, there'll be a small passage written fairly early on that becomes a source of encouragement for me: a paragraph or two, usually, reading exactly the way I want the whole book to read. I'll loop back to this passage time and time again, telling myself that one day the whole book will be as strong and moving as it. That's the little bit of living impulse Eisenberg talks about. However that impulse manifests in your novel, hold tight to it while also forgiving yourself everything else in your book that isn't yet as strong. Remember that your first draft is meant, first and foremost, to be exploratory, playful, and generative, a process of discovery and creation: you are learning what your story is and who your characters are; you are making the materials you'll need later to revise and rewrite your novel into a better, truer version of itself.

Jane Smiley helpfully divides the kinds of sentences you write in this exploratory draft into seeds and pebbles, saying, "If it's a pebble, it's just the next sentence and it sits there. But if it's a seed it grows into something that becomes an important part of the life of the novel. The problem is, you can't know ahead of time whether a sentence will be a seed or a pebble, or how important a seed it's going to be."

You write your way through a field of pebbles, looking for seeds. They will be there, hiding among everything else. But the pebbles and the seeds are yours; you made them both, by your own wit and ingenuity, by your work ethic and your daily habits and your refusal to flinch or give up.

Forgive the pebbles, gather your seeds. The second draft awaits.

SECOND DRAFT:
Rewrite, Don't Revise

CELEBRATE THE ROUGH ROUGH DRAFT

One day, you will emerge from the long, sustained work of your exploratory first draft to discover that you've at last reached the end. Congratulations!

Whether this is your first novel or your tenth, take the time to celebrate. Let yourself linger in your accomplishment. Writing hundreds of pages of prose is an incredible feat all its own, and in those pages is, you hope, a first version of the story you wanted to tell, populated by meaningful events in the lives of characters you've come to know and truly care about.

You may reach this moment in a state of pure bliss or profound despair. You may see only what is right and good about the book or only what is broken and in need of repair. You may, if you're like me, swing between these two ends of the emotional spectrum, unsure if you've written a great novel or a terrible one.

You may also be uncertain if what you've written is, in fact, a novel at all. You might only know that whatever this draft is, it's *done*, leaving nothing more to be gained from working on it in this form, in this way.

Good. Good! Congratulations again!

I finished the first draft of my first novel in a mad rush of creative energy. I hadn't known exactly what would happen at the end until I was about thirty pages away from it, when it came to me all at once. I stopped where I was, leapt forward, and wrote the last ten pages in a single go—pages that, unlike everything else in the book, would turn out to barely have to be edited later—and then returned to the place I'd left off and worked my way to the island of that ending. I finished on a summer afternoon in Michigan, then went outside and crashed into my backyard lawn, clutching a drink and feeling simultaneously elated and crushed.

I was done.

I was not done.

I sat on the ground, resting between these two truths, and thought, *What now?*

What a First Draft Is and Is Not

You celebrate for as long as you possibly can, and then one day you reopen your Word document or your notebook full of ink-stained pages.

Even before you look, you know what you will find there will be *rough*, in the fullest sense of what we mean by *rough draft*. This is nothing to be dismayed about, although perhaps you'll be dismayed anyway, as I always am. But the first draft isn't the book I'm writing, only a sort of one-to-one scale model of it, not the novel itself but an idea of what the novel could be. I always think here of the Jorges Luis Borges story "On Exactitude in Science," where a country's caste of cartographers pursues accuracy and excellence to the point of creating a highly detailed map exactly the same size as the country, an impressive but entirely useless artifact.

In the Borges story, the country-size map is eventually allowed to blow away into the desert, where its tattered scraps become inhabited by "animals and beggars." Nothing quite so dramatic has happened to any of my early attempts, but it remains true that the first drafts of my novels have never been the real thing, only full-scale suggestions of what they might become. Book-size maps of books.

The second draft we're about to embark upon aims to produce the book your book-size map suggests, something much closer to the ideal novel you set out to write. We do this by a process of *narrative revision* and *rewriting*.

Take a Break

But first, put the novel in a drawer. Swear off opening your Word document. After months or years of drafting, you need to put two kinds of time between you and the manuscript: *lived time* and *art time*.

Lived time is exactly what it sounds like. Give yourself a month or two months or six months—whatever it takes to get the novel out of your daily thoughts, so you can come back to it fresh. It doesn't take long for something that once consumed you to feel impossibly distant. After the months of staying close to your manuscript, keeping it in your mind and your heart so your brain worked on it even when you were not at your desk, now's the time to reverse the process. Ideally, you eventually arrive at a point where you're no longer thinking of the book much at all.

Paradoxically, once this happens, you're halfway to being ready to dive back in again.

The other half of your break is something you can do simultaneously. While your novel is resting, *write something else*. Put some art time between you and the book so you can return as a slightly different writer, excited about new things. Writing in a fresh voice or perspective will return you to your novel draft with the distance you need to see the manuscript for what it is, in its present form, and will also help you imagine possibilities for what it might become.

Give yourself the break the novel needs you to take. It's as Hilary Mantel once said: "I have to take a deep breath before I start the first full revision. I used to hate myself for procrastinating, but now I see it might be wise. You need to pause in holy fear at what you've done, and make sure you don't wreck it in panic."

OUTLINING THE FIRST DRAFT TO FIND THE SECOND

After you've achieved some distance, you'll be ready to reread the novel to rediscover what your material is. It's at this stage—and never before this stage—that I write a full outline of the novel, outlining *what already exists*. You can do this however you want: in traditional outline form; in a bullet-point list; on index cards tacked to your office wall conspiracy-theorist style, with strings connecting narrative threads; or as a beat sheet or set of storyboards. Or, you could outline as I do, which is to write a *narrative outline*, a summary of the book written in an approximation of the novel's voice. (Why write your outline in the voice of the novel? For me, it helps this planning to feel more like *writing*, and it keeps my thinking closer to the novel's sensibilities.)

In this document, the goal is to try to capture the main story of the novel, by which I mean the action of the book's prime timeline. What you want to get down in this outline are the book's *events*, a term Anna Keesey usefully defines as "everything that progresses time in the narrative." In other words, not interiority, not digression, not backstory—just what *happens*.

As you write your outline, study the cause-and-effect relationship between events, the "beats" in the story where time progresses and where action unfolds. Look for what Jim Shepard calls the *rate of revelation*, "the sense we have of the pace at which we're learning crucial emotional information about the stories' central figures." How long does it take to get to the novel's inciting incident? How frequently does something new happen? Where are the events that change the reader's understanding or raise tension or advance conflict?

Where is the turn to the ending? Which threads are brought to a clear conclusion in the final pages of the novel, and which are left unresolved?

By doing this, you'll likely discover which actions and choices drove the plot of the first draft, which are easier to see once divorced from exposition and interiority and backstory. You may also find spans where you're summarizing or digressing too often, stalling out the plot's action; or places where crucial actions are missing entirely.

Take your time with this document. Even if you made your first draft from a prewriting outline, that early outline likely no longer corresponds to the book you've actually written. Your job here is to make a model of your novel, as it exists right now; for the next step in the process to work well, you want this model to be as accurate as possible.

Revise the Outline into a Plan

Once my outline is complete, I revise it, not the novel, until the outline becomes a plan for the better book I want to write. This is one way of revising the action of the novel at a macro level, without having to deal with all the minutiae. Anyone who's ever tried to reorganize a book manuscript by moving ten-page chunks of prose knows how daunting that quickly becomes: it can be difficult to commit yourself to radical but necessary change when you know it means rewriting every single sentence to make the moved material fit into its new home.

We're still going to have to do this work, but for now, we're pretending it's going to be easy—in part, by making it as easy as it can be.

Start by analyzing the novel's plot as it's expressed in the new outline. How is your story shaped? Do you have a clear three-act structure? Are you loosely following the familiar inciting incident/rising action/climax/denouement shape of Freytag's Pyramid? Are you doing something less linear, something more associative or otherwise unconventional? Jane Alison's recent *Meander, Spiral, Explode* shows a number of less traditional ways novels might be shaped, many of them mimicking patterns found in the natural world: the wave, the cell network, the fractal. There are so many possible ways to structure your story, and certainly there's no one right answer. The aim here is to discover what you've already done and then think of how you might better take advantage of the inherent qualities in the structure you've chosen.

You might also have to choose a different structure. I frequently have.

Many novels begin in the stasis of a status quo, which is broken by the inciting incident that kicks off the story. Can you identify this moment? If not, you probably have a problem: for most conventional plot shapes, the inciting incident has to be clear, and it has to happen in the scene, on the page. Once your inciting incident is clearly established, study how the scenes that follow work to introduce us to your novel's cast and your setting, while simultaneously kicking off the rising action of the plot. How efficient can you make these scenes? Where can you usefully merge discovery scenes and forward action so that we emerge as quickly and powerfully as possible from the introduction of the story into the main event?

One way to determine if the transition out of the status quo is well placed is to identify the first moment where characters stop *reacting* to the inciting incident and start *enacting* solutions to the problems it has caused. There are no hard-and-fast rules on where this changeover from acting to enacting might happen—you might right now be thinking of a counterexample where it successfully and movingly never happens—but many good novels you've read do possess such a moment, skillfully placed. Find where your turn currently is and then adjust, if necessary. If you've written a four-hundred-page novel and this enacting doesn't start until page two hundred, you might have an issue. If you've written a three-hundred-page book and the enacting begins on page eighty, it might be perfectly positioned.

If it never happens, well, that's why you're revising your narrative outline. Better to know it (and fix it) now before committing to a full second draft.

Another test I'm constantly applying to my plots, no matter how they're shaped, comes from Robert McKee's *Story*, in which McKee writes that "a story must not retreat to actions of lesser quality or magnitude, but move progressively forward to a final action beyond which the audience cannot imagine another." Regardless of the kind of structure you've chosen, this test can often be applied: as the novel progresses, ask yourself if the quality and importance of events, scenes, reveals, and complications continue to climb. If not, why not, and how might your material be rearranged to make the climb more apparent?

Move events around and try out different combinations, paying special attention to the effect your moves have on the book's causality. Chains of cause and effect are at the root of how readers make sense of most narratives—good, clear causality creates easily understood stakes, suspense, and payoffs. So, it's a good idea to make sure the logic between events is scannable to you at this phase.

While you're doing this, keep an eye out for unproductive doublings. Sometimes an event repeats or rhymes to good effect, but often there's a sense of diminishing returns, especially if the event isn't somehow of higher quality or intensity. Whenever I find I've written two versions of a particular action where I need only one, I cut one or (more often) combine the best parts of both into a single, more vivid event—or I take advantage of the iterative possibilities of a well-designed progressive series of scenes to expand the sequence, as described in the last chapter.

Revising your new outline to discover the next version of your book is one way to help yourself imagine big changes with ease, because you're revising a sentence instead of a scene, a paragraph instead of a chapter. This can be a time-consuming process, but all the work you do here is going to pay off in the months to come. The goal is to end up with an outline that's less a document of what exists and more a plan for the better book you want the second draft to be, discovered among the material of the first draft's more organic creation.

Once you begin the second draft of your novel (more on this in a few pages), you'll use this outline as a guide for what to write and as a reference to what you've already written. At many stages of the process, it'll be useful to be able to scan the entirety of your plot at once, something more easily accomplished with an outline than with a full read-through of the novel. So, spend as much time as it takes here to make this outline the best it can be.

For my first novel, writing and revising the outline took a couple of weeks. For *Appleseed*, my most recent, it took three months, in part because I was juggling three timelines that had to work on their own and then meaningfully intersect. In both cases, the narrative outline saved me so much time and effort later that I would gladly have spent twice as long doing it if that's what it would have taken to do it right.

How to Outline Multiple Storylines

If your novel has three storylines braided together, should you outline them separately or individually? My guess is either could work, but for me it's worked best to outline each thread as if it were its own book, then revise those individual outlines before rebraiding the storylines back together.

Each individual storyline probably needs to have its own interior logic while simultaneously working with the others to create a single rising action that carries the reader through the novel. Additionally, you'll likely need to find ways to match the pace of the conflict and the rate of revelation across the storylines, especially if they're all of about the same length. The end of act one in storyline B usually can't occur fifty pages after the act-ending action in storyline A, and so on. Taking the time to do this planning at this outline stage might save you work later by keeping you from designing storylines of vastly varied paces, which could translate into vastly different page counts.

But what if you do end up with storylines of different lengths? Then you'll either have to even them out or find a way to make the difference into an opportunity. I've already mentioned the three timelines in my novel *Appleseed*: after my second draft, they were each book length on their own, with the first two coming in at sixty thousand words each and the third at a slightly slimmer forty thousand. Figuring out how to braid them back together without writing another twenty thousand words for the third timeline was a challenge, but not having more of that timeline to play with ended up being a constraint that pushed me toward a more interesting structure than I'd originally planned.

NOW REWRITE THE NOVEL

By which I mean, *now write the novel.*

Here's the part of my personal process no one ever wants to hear about but that is, in my mind, the most necessary and productive thing I do, the real way I transition from the mess of the first draft to the tighter, better-made second draft: I retype my second draft from scratch, rewriting as I go, moving the book I've already drafted toward the one described by the outline I've spent the last weeks or months crafting.

If you want to do this, feel free to use the first draft as a guide—I use two monitors at home, and I put the first draft on one monitor while I type the second draft on the other—but whatever you do, don't cut and paste to save time.

Instead, retype everything.

Yes, everything.

In an interview, Amy Tan once said, "Only when I finish the book can I go back to the beginning and write in the voice of all that happened." This is your goal for the second draft: to rewrite your novel in the "voice of all that happened," with a knowledge of what the story is and of who your characters are, knowledge you simply could not have possessed on the day you started your first draft.

The earliest pages you wrote will have a certain energy to them that you'll want to feed on, but often the voice of the novel grows into itself over the months or years of drafting it takes to produce a first draft. Therefore, the trick of the second draft is to recapture or re-create the magic that inspired the novel in the first place, but to do so with the fullness of the style you developed by the time you reached the end. More than anything else, committing to this process will divorce you from the sentences you wrote while you were figuring out what your novel was, making way for new prose written with a fuller understanding of who your characters are, of what their story is, and of how the story might best be shaped.

If you use the two-monitor setup (or re-create it with a tablet or a printout), delete or cross out any material you've used from the first draft once it's been transferred and rewritten into the second. (Again, don't cut and paste, if you can avoid it: you'll find it unbearable to retype a bad sentence, but you won't be as hard on anything you copy.) As you rewrite, you'll inevitably improve the prose, making slightly different choices as you rewrite, and retyping the whole novel makes it much easier to make the necessary changes at the level of plot and character. In this way, the first draft becomes what I call a *diminishing draft*. One day, the diminishing draft will be depleted down to nothing, while your second draft will have grown from a blank document into the better novel you planned in your revised narrative outline.

Earlier in the process, I encouraged you to feel free to write nonlinearly, to write in fragments, to go wherever you wanted in your novel at any time. In this draft, I suggest you work more linearly, staying with each scene until it's as done as it can be. Get the action right, build your characters as fully as possible, push hard on your prose. If a scene seems impossible to write, take some time and think about why: Is the scene merely hard to write, or are you writing the wrong scene altogether?

Adjust your outline as you go, keeping it in line with the

work you're doing: anywhere you deviate from the outline, adjust the plan for what comes after.

The process I've suggested here does require you to physically make every sentence and paragraph and scene and chapter again, which is admittedly an incredible effort. Usually, this second draft takes me the same amount of time the first draft did, so a year-long first draft begets a year-long second draft. But the quality of the work is often startlingly different: characters come more alive when put into action in scenes better designed to reveal them and test them; events link together into more believable (and more surprising) chains of cause and effect. There will still be plenty of discovery in this draft, but the raw confusion of *what book am I writing?* will recede as you become surer and surer of what it is you're making.

I frequently teach a graduate novel workshop where, in addition to our writing, we read novels by contemporary writers who later visit us virtually or in person to answer questions about their process. So many award-winning, bestselling writers have told us that they also start over and write fresh for the second draft. Some work off their first draft, like I do, while others put the first draft in a drawer and never look back, knowing they have the story under control and can now focus on making the best possible version of it.

Like these writers, I've found this is a crucial aspect of my process: it wasn't until the second draft of each of my novels was completed that I felt I had written a *book*. Despite the difficulty and the time commitment, I can't recommend this whole novel rewrite enough; it can be a truly transformative experience. As Robert Boswell once said, "I don't write to polish, but to permit the narrative to move away from my initial intentions, to become complex and strange—or at least not boring. I call each of these changing versions a transitional draft, and I don't quit until the story stands on its own hooves and turns around to glower—meaning that it's fully alive and no longer mine."

That's the goal of this rewrite: to work until the book you're writing becomes the book it wants to be, uniquely itself, fully alive. This second-draft rewrite from scratch (or close to it) is the surest way I've found to make this happen. It's also my major piece of advice for the second draft of the novel, which, if my experience is anything to go by, will most often produce the first real and proper draft of the book your novel has always wanted to become.

THE FIRST GUIDING PRINCIPLE

There are two guiding principles to this book, neither of which I've explicitly stated so far. Here's the first one, which guides my second drafts and, in truth, my entire process: *When in doubt, rewrite instead of revise.*

How do you know if you're *rewriting* versus *revising*?

Some clues: the presence of new typing (or at least retyping) and the absence of merely copying and pasting.

When in doubt, rewrite instead of revise.

Trust me.

NOW YOU'VE WRITTEN A BOOK (AGAIN, AND ALSO FOR THE FIRST TIME)

One day, likely months after you've finished your narrative outline and set up your diminishing draft and then started rewriting your novel into the seeming abyss of another blank document, you'll once again reach the end.

Congratulations!

You've done it! Celebrate! Call your partner or a friend and exclaim into the telephone. Discover new and more joyous emojis in your writers' group chat. Treat yourself to a meal or a drink or a hike or a nap. Then take another break: art time, lived time. Make something new, do something different, try out new and different makings and doings until you feel the necessary distance again.

If you want, this might be a good time to give the book to a first reader. But if you can wait, do. Your friends love you, but they're going to read your novel only so many times. The longer you can hold off, the higher-level feedback you'll receive, because so much will already be working that only what you couldn't figure out yourself will remain.

That said, there's nothing wrong with not waiting. Hearing someone else talk about their experience of reading your book might be the encouragement you need to persevere into the next draft. If you think that might be the case, go for it.

If you do have a friend read the novel at this stage, I'd suggest holding off on asking for much line-level or concrete feedback, because you're going to address a lot of the work yourself in the next draft anyway. What might be most encouraging and helpful is to ask your first readers simply to give you an hour of their time, in person or on the phone or over Zoom. During this conversation, listen more than you speak. Give your first readers space to tell you what they liked, to enthuse about their favorite parts of the plot and what they loved about your characters, and more than anything else, to give you the great gift of seeing your story living in someone else's heart and mind. You can live a long time on joy like that. It might even sustain you all the way to the end of the third and final draft you're about to begin.

THIRD DRAFT:

Refuse to be Done

THE SECOND GUIDING PRINCIPLE

So, you've finished your second draft! The manuscript in front of you is broadly complete: the characters are fleshed out, the plot holds together beginning to end, and your first readers have assured you that the sentences are indeed readable.

Now what?

Now we reach the second guiding principle of this book: *Refuse to be done.*

What you want now is to stay inside your novel as long as possible, giving yourself every chance to transform this pretty good draft into a novel that's as great as it can be.

Most of what I'll advocate for in the pages to come is a "layered" approach to revision: instead of tackling every problem area or opportunity in your manuscript simultaneously, you'll break the work into smaller tasks meant to be done one at a time, one after another.

While you're doing this small work, page after page, pass

after pass, you'll inevitably be improving the whole novel. The activities in this chapter will give you a way to stay in the work long enough to manifest yourself upon the page not once or twice but dozens or hundreds of times, until you end up not with a book written by the you who existed on any particular day but, rather, one collaborated upon by the many selves who existed over the likely hundreds of days you were writing. These daily manifestations—the many versions of the writer that have come together to collaborate upon the work—are what, I believe, makes our favorite books seem written by superhumans, full of that "incomprehensible abundance" Smiley described.

These "genius" books really are better than what any one of us could write on any individual day, but that's not how they were written. As we fill our hours and days with the work of rewriting, our fictions will not be written by any one self but by the spectrum of selves we're always becoming, even as the novel is becoming alongside us.

EDITING: SCREEN OR PRINT?

If you've reached this late stage of the writing process working entirely on your computer or another device, I recommend printing out the draft to hold its heft in your hands—there's true joy in feeling the weight of a novel's worth of your own prose for the first time—and to give yourself another way back into the work. The mode of the screen is not reading line by line but skimming or scrolling—watch someone interact with Twitter or Instagram, or pay attention to your own eyes and hands as you read an article online. But we don't want to skim or scroll through our drafts. Revising and rewriting on paper will slow you down, keep you closer to the words. It won't be the only way you edit, but it deserves to be a part of the process.

Still, word processing software offers obvious advantages, especially the ease of moving chunks of prose from one part of a book to another. (At this stage, I usually lift my second-draft ban on copying and pasting.) Some of the processes and operations I'll suggest in the pages to come might work better in one medium than the other, but proceed in whatever way is most comfortable. Just remember that there's power in making something feel new again. If you find yourself stuck or bored, try switching your tools. Trade in the pen and paper for the laptop and the mouse, or vice versa. Finding ways to vary the texture of the work is likely one of the keys to maintaining the necessary perseverance to see yourself through the process of refusing to be done.

READ ALOUD OFTEN

For similar reasons, I can't advocate strongly enough for reading aloud from the manuscript on a daily basis. Your ear will hear what your eyes won't see. You have to read every word when you read aloud, something you don't have to do when reading silently on the page or the screen, where you'll naturally skim, especially as you get overused to your own prose. Additionally, your ear will catch possibilities you might not find while reading silently: as you fix the music of your prose, you may find you inadvertently fix the sense, too.

Even better might be finding a friend or fellow writer willing to read your prose back to you, so you can more purely listen. In addition to all the hands-on editing you're doing at this stage, it's great to find ways to experience the book without your red pen at the ready. I've never been so lucky as to have a friend willing to read me to me—or else I've been too Midwestern to impose—but I have used the text-to-speech function on my Mac to turn my Word document into a robot-voiced audiobook, which I then listened to on long drives in the car. If you want a brutal test of how well your prose is holding up, I promise that a tone-deaf robot with pronunciation issues will be happy to give you the least generous read possible.

BREAK THE PROSE INTO MANAGEABLE CHUNKS

I often privilege sound in exploratory drafts and then move toward sense: I need a sentence to sound good before I can move on, need a story to have a voice before it can have characters or plot or anything else—but then I have to revisit all those good-sounding sentences to make sure they make sense. Music is wonderful, but clarity is essential, too. One way I work on both music and clarity together is to break the prose into smaller units. This way the goal isn't to "perfect" the entire book, only this scene, this paragraph, this sentence. All my techniques for the third draft are means of doing this: what I want more than anything is to isolate one aspect of the novel at a time, thus making the day's goal small enough to be achievable.

One technique I often employ is to temporarily put a page break after every scene in my manuscript. When I print out the book, I leave the page breaks in so I can easily rearrange scenes, shuffling the story into a new order, remembering that the order in which information is delivered to the reader is one of the primary contributors to the building and release of tension. I wonder: Is there another way my scenes or chapters might be arranged that maximizes the tension, raises the stakes, or more clearly demonstrates causality? This rearranging work might both uncover missing pieces of plot and help you figure out where those missing pieces might go.

Sometimes revising scene by scene means still working with too big a unit. If a particular chapter or scene isn't working, try putting every paragraph on its own page, if only inside your word processor. (All those printed pages add up!) I learned this tactic from Don DeLillo's *Paris Review* interview, in which he talked about writing his novel *The Names*. DeLillo said,

"When I finished a paragraph, even a three-line paragraph, I automatically went to a fresh page to start the new paragraph. No crowded pages. This enabled me to see a given set of sentences more clearly . . . The white space on the page helped me concentrate more deeply on what I'd written."

DeLillo was using a *typewriter* to do this: imagine all that white space of his physical pages surrounding all those typewritten paragraphs. Even on the screen you'll find it surprisingly satisfying to let your paragraphs stand as their own units in this way before you recombine them into longer passages and scenes and chapters. (Not that you have to stitch them together: plenty of novels have been built entirely of single-paragraph pages or extremely short sections, like Joe Wenderoth's *Letters to Wendy's*.) If you're feeling ambitious—or masochistic—you could do this with individual sentences. Cut a page into its pieces, throw away whatever's unable to stand on its own, then reassemble what's left, writing between sentences wherever something new seems to be required.

Chances are you'll end up with something stronger than you began with; if not, it's easy enough to restore the original version if you've been using Track Changes, as I've suggested elsewhere. Ideally, when you put everything back together, it will be in a new and better order than the one in which you originally wrote it. There's a lot of opportunity in your being willing to move everything: chapters, scenes, paragraphs, sentences, clauses within sentences, words within clauses. You'll be amazed at how many paragraphs and sentences don't need rewriting, just radical rearranging.

I like doing this rearranging with a printed manuscript, but this is also where software like Scrivener shines. One of its best features is how easy it makes it to shuffle scenes and chapters into new configurations and to see the structure of your book on the screen at a glance. I've personally not had a lot of luck writing fiction in Scrivener, but I did write *this* book in it. Different tools work better for different kinds of projects, and trying new software might be another way to break a logjam in your work.

SCENE STRUCTURE

At this stage, you want to be sure your novel's scenes are doing the plot work you need them to do: page after page, conflicts are introduced, resolutions are sought, complications arise and are dealt with, making way for new conflicts and new complications, and so on. From here on out, the task is figuring out less *what happens* and more *the best way to show it happening*.

The next few operations are ways of making your scenes as tight and concise as they can be and considering how the information in each scene is organized. How do you get the reader in and out as efficiently as possible? How do you move the reader's imagination through the scene, showing them what matters most?

Cut the Opening and Closing Paragraphs of Scenes

In 2012, Matthew Salesses curated "A Month of Revision" at *Necessary Fiction*, an event he kicked off with an incredibly practical list of personal revision tactics. One of those was a radical revision technique I'd never heard of before but that I've since found incredibly useful: "Cut the opening paragraph. Cut the last paragraph. Do that for each scene. Now rewrite the ones that have to be there, let the rest die." (An expanded version of Salesses's list can be found in his excellent book *Craft in the Real World*.) This works well in part because it addresses one of the most common pieces of feedback given in writing workshops: if you've spent any time in such classrooms, you've likely seen your share of stories that seem to get started only on page 3 or that dribble on a bit past what seems like the strongest ending.

Salesses's suggestion is a bit of a brute-force hack, but it can be done with purpose: feel free to turn on Track Changes to make the operation feel less alarming. Once you've lopped off the opening and closing paragraphs of your scenes, go back and read each scene. Sometimes, the scene will already be improved by starting later and ending earlier, but other times you'll find you've cut away something vital. As you rewrite these openings and closings, you'll be working with a better understanding of how the scenes work than when you first drafted them.

If this technique works for you, feel free to try it more than once. You may be surprised at how many times it can fruitfully be repeated.

Consider How the Camera Moves Through a Scene

In each scene, consider how the camera or the "eye" of the scene moves the reader through the visuals on offer: Does the description begin zoomed out and then move closer in? Does it progress in a way that makes it easy for the reader to imagine? A default mode of movement might be top to bottom, left to right, big to small, moving as your eyes might move, taking in a new room or a new location (or a new page). If scene-setting description is presented without some kind of order, it becomes disorientingly cubist, with details appearing disconnected or overlapping, difficult to order—and while this effect might be usefully employed, you should be sure that's what you're trying to do.

Clearly Mark Transitions in Time and Space

Timelines are the bane of many a novelist. Early on, they're often provisional, if not outright ignored. During a first draft, I don't always know what season my story is taking place in, so I write some scenes in which it's snowing, others where it's sunny and bright, with my characters dressing incongruously for weather that might or might not come. Eventually, though, all this has to be smoothed out and made clear. By the third draft, you've likely done most of this timeline work already—ideally, during the second draft's outlining and rewriting—but you need to be sure the reader can follow along.

As a writer who cares deeply about the sound of his sentences, I used to resist time and setting tags, which are most often written in the plainest prose. But how much time has passed since the last chapter is vital information: if readers leave a scene and skip forward a decade, they expect a totally different kind of scene than if the novel skips forward only ten minutes.

Anthony Doerr's long short story "The Caretaker" is unusually complex, taking place in Liberia and Oregon (and, briefly, in between), covering not months but years. Doerr's prose is on the more lyrical end of the spectrum, begging you to pay attention to its sound and syntax, but this doesn't prevent him from doing the work of moving you expertly and efficiently through time and space. Here are some time/space indicators from the story's first few pages, which often also announce the duration of events:

"For his first thirty-five years . . . [Joseph lives] in a small, collapsing house in the hills outside Monrovia in Liberia, West Africa."

"In 1989 Liberia descends into a civil war that will last seven years."

"In October of 1994 . . ."

"The next night . . ."

"In the days to come . . ."

"After a month . . ."

"After several minutes . . ."

"He wakes on the floor inside the plantation house . . ."

"He boards a chemical tanker . . ."

"He disembarks in Astoria, Oregon . . ."

So much movement in so few pages! The cost of this kind of clear marking of time and space is no more than a handful of words, words the reader will read quickly and move past. The payoff is immense: the reader will be able to put events in relation to one another, to more clearly understand the cause and effect between them, and they will anticipate different kinds of suspense and tension at different scales of time. It would be possible to write a version of "The Caretaker" in which Doerr used jump cuts to move between the events, but it would likely not be a *better* version.

Ted Chiang's novella "The Lifecycle of Software Objects" covers an even longer span of time than "The Caretaker," with Chiang taking similar pains to ensure that the reader knows how much time has passed between scenes. The story moves from the real world into virtual spaces, includes scenes driven by email threads and chat boards, and covers not only years but decades. Over 110 pages, almost every section begins with a marker of passing time: "a year later," "within the first year," "over the next year," "over the course of the following year," "after another year has gone by," "a month later," "another year passes," "two more years pass." Note how similar these markers are: they're not novelties but clarities. Likely, the reader doesn't linger on them at all, but that doesn't mean they're not hugely important to the overall effect of Chiang's novella.

THE MYSTERIOUS ART OF CHAPTERING

What is the ideal length of a novel chapter?

No one knows. But some suggestive trends are to be found in contemporary literature. Here's a sample of chapter lengths from novels off the top of my to-be-read pile, all published in the months preceding this writing: Susan Steinberg's *Machine*, with chapters ranging between ten and fifteen pages; Amanda Goldblatt's *Hard Mouth*, which opens with a ten-page chapter followed by an eighty-page one; Margaret Atwood's *The Testaments*, which has both a four-page chapter and a thirty-five-page one; Amitav Ghosh's *Gun Island*, whose chapters run ten to thirty pages; and Marlon James's *Black Leopard, Red Wolf*, whose shortest division listed in the table of contents is twelve pages and whose longest runs for one hundred fifty, with the book altogether comprising twenty-four numbered chapters of approximately equal length. And then there are the novels of extremes, like Lucy Ellmann's recent *Ducks, Newburyport*, which contains a single sentence that spans a thousand pages, or Kathryn Scanlan's *Aug 9— Fog*, which usually has fewer than fifty words to a page.

If I had to guess, I'd say the average contemporary novel has chapters ranging somewhere between ten and twenty pages in length, with the possibility of incredible variation both within and between books. For some time now, the overall trend has been toward shorter chapters, especially in literary fiction, and more so in novels with what might be called lyrical language. Victor LaValle's *The Changeling*, for instance, has 103 chapters, many of which are only a page or two in length, a feature that likely contributes to how fast that novel reads, despite being more than four hundred pages long.

You may not have such a clear idea about how your own chaptering works—I tend to test many different strategies before landing on the final arrangement—but it's worth trying to articulate your method so far. Why is your novel organized the way it is? How many storylines are you juggling? If you have multiple protagonists, how long can you follow one before we need to check in with another?

Perhaps more important than the raw length of your chapters is what they ask of your reader and how they guide the reader through the story. Given the complexities of your plot, the density of your language, and the intensity of the events depicted, how often might your reader need a rest, whether that's a line of white space between sections or a fuller page break between chapters? What other effects might white space and page breaks create in your narrative? But keep in mind that what creates a rest in one book might arrive as a shock in another.

While you're working through these choices, be sure to reserve some time to revisit the endings of your chapters after you're done rearranging. My sense is most writers put slightly more effort into their openings while drafting, possibly because reaching the end of a chapter is such a relief that we rush to the page break as soon as we can. This is a good time to make sure your endings are as strong as they can be and to see if there are new opportunities for revision suggested by the structural changes you've been making.

Try Removing Section Breaks (Without Changing Anything Else)

One of the last things I did to my novel *Appleseed* in manuscript was to go through and take out as many section breaks within chapters as I could, deleting the white space and other markings between them. (By *section break*, I mean the smaller divisions of text that sometimes exist within chapters, usually set off by a string of three asterisks or something similar.) Late in my revision, I found that many of these mid-chapter breaks, all of which had seemed so essential, had become unnecessary and that losing those interruptions let my chapters read as more continuous and seamless. Obviously, many books get great work out of tiny sections or fragments, including favorites of mine like Renata Adler's *Speedboat* and Jenny Offill's *Dept. of Speculation*. If you're writing this kind of book, carry on! But if you're writing a more conventionally chaptered book, give this tactic a try. You'll be surprised how often you won't have to do anything to transition smoothly between the newly joined sections, while other times you'll find that merely adding a minor transitional phrase will be enough to erase any evidence of the former break.

PROSE STYLE

At last, it's time to talk sentences—but why did we wait so long to work the prose in the first place?

Because until now, we've had bigger concerns. Maybe you were writing a multigenerational saga of war and betrayal, trying to hold forty-seven characters in your head at once—it's okay if you dangled a participle somewhere along the way to figuring out that plot or accidentally employed the most cliché of clichés in introducing your massive cast. Still, for many writers, allowing for a productive looseness in the prose during early drafts is one of the most mentally demanding parts of novel writing, particularly because we often emphasize the pure quality of our prose as a marker of being a "real" writer.

I'm as guilty of this as anyone. One of the truest joys of writing is the pleasure of moving language around on the page, endeavoring to make a narrative voice feel alive and surprising. Certainly, I always try to write the best sentences I can. But because I know I'm inevitably going to rewrite so much of every novel—and throw away so much of what I labored so hard over early in the process—I also try not to get too precious too early, leaving the final tune-up of my prose for later.

Even if you're the kind of writer who can't move forward until a page is *perfect*, you may benefit from some of the following tricks and tactics. You can employ them as you go, or you can wait to work through the entire manuscript after it's otherwise feature-complete.

Work the Verbs

Scene by scene, look at the verbs you've chosen: Are they the best verbs, the most active, the most surprising? Or are they more pedestrian, everyday, overly mundane? Replacing even some of the most typical verbs with more precise and interesting ones will lift the level of your prose.

Benjamin Percy's fiction is a great model for studying the effect of well-chosen, often visceral verbs. In the prologue of his novel *Red Moon*, a security guard "spotlights" a driver's license with a flashlight; passengers "wobble" down the aisle of a plane; a throat is "excised" in an airborne werewolf attack at thirty thousand feet. Blood "spatters," which is expected, but also "decorates," which is not. A brave flight attendant "under-hands" a carafe of coffee at an attacker, futilely wielding it as a weapon.

It's not too hard to imagine the less interesting verbs that might have been: the guard could have "looked at" the license, the passengers could have "walked" down the aisle, and so on. Sometimes a showier verb can be a bit much, but consider what you might use in place of any verb that feels so obvious it verges on the default. Your verbs are literally the most active part of your sentences, the place where the action occurs. More often than not, the more interesting the verb, the more interesting the action.

There's one notable exception to this advice: dialogue tags. Here, the most commonly used verbs, *said* and *asked*, will be the right choice most of the time, precisely because they're so unremarkable. *Said* and *asked* do the work of ensuring that the reader isn't confused about who's saying what, and then they get out of the way, leaving the focus on what's being said. Other choices can be made for deliberate effect, but you shouldn't feel pressured to vary from *said* and other common dialogue tags (or to modify them with adverbs) merely for variety's sake.

Diminish Thought Tags

One category of verb you might be able to dramatically reduce are those indicating that a character is thinking: I *thought*, he *wondered*, she *understood*, they *knew*. In first-person prose, we're already inside the character's speech and thoughts, so these tags are usually unnecessary: so much of what is on the page is thought that we'll read the rest that way, too. And in close third person (especially the mode James Wood calls "free indirect style"), the narrator's diction and syntax are related enough that thoughts can be rendered without the tags and a savvy reader will know how to read them.

Use the Find function to search for each of the words I've just mentioned, as they appear in the particular tense of your novel. When you find a usage, delete the tag, then reread the paragraph in which it appears. If it's clear that the recently untagged sentence or clause is a thought, you're all set. If it's not clear, rewrite the sentence to make it so without restoring the tag. These thought tags mediate the experience between the narrator and the writer; removing them allows the reader to experience the thought directly, without interruption. More often than not, that's the stronger choice.

Diminish Sensory Verbs

You can also get rid of many verbs used to indicate that a character is looking at something: I *saw*, I *looked*, I *watched*. Cut those verbs and describe the thing being seen. Where you wrote, "she looked at the approaching car," try "the car approached," and so on. In the first person, we're already inside the narrator's perspective: everything described is something they're looking at. The same principle applies most of the time in second or third person, because we're right there with the characters, seeing what they're seeing.

After you finish searching for looking verbs, do another pass for verbs indicating hearing. As we saw with the looking verbs, changing "he heard a dog barking" to "a dog barked" will make the prose move faster and will eliminate the mediating layer of the character, allowing the reader to "hear" for themselves more directly.

It'll be less of an issue, but you can often do the same for the other senses. Tasting and touching verbs are more active and might stay, but most of the time "smelled" can go. Whenever possible, go directly to describing the image, the sound, the flavor, the aroma, the sensation. The result will be faster, more immediate prose that delivers all the key sensory detail directly to the reader.

Diminish "To Be"

The various forms of *to be* (*be*, *is*, *am*, *are*, *was*, *were*, *been*, and *being*) are necessary and important parts of the English language, and in certain kinds of purposely flat or cold styles, they provide much of the intended effect. But for most prose styles, you might find you can profitably reduce the number of times you use them. Sometimes this verb indicates that a sentence is currently in the passive voice, when you might be better off attaching the action described to a character ("the bomb is being defused" becomes "Angela defuses the bomb"); other times they indicate habitual actions or a static moment that might be better off happening within a single beat of narrative time ("we were fighting the dragon" becomes "we fought the dragon"). Sometimes they're simply unnecessary: "We wanted to rob the casino that was owned by the unscrupulous land developer" can more concisely be written as "We wanted to rob the casino owned by the unscrupulous land developer," or, even better, "We wanted to rob the unscrupulous land developer's casino."

Another unnecessary usage is what's called an *expletive construction*—look for "there is," "there are," "there were"—which can be fixed simply by finding the stronger subject within the existing sentence and giving it a better verb to work with: "There were several new clues in the starlet's hotel room" could be written as "The starlet's hotel room offered up several new clues."

Searching for the various forms of *to be* will give you another way to see your prose anew, allowing you to continue to improve what can be improved. But note that there are plenty of reasons you might use *to be*: the goal here isn't to eliminate it entirely, only to be sure you're always using the strongest verb you can, on your way to making the best sentence possible.

Vary Sentence and Paragraph Lengths

Way back during the first draft, I suggested that one kind of playful interruption you might practice is to revise with an eye to varying your sentence lengths in dramatic ways, which would create new effects and opportunities for drama. I suggest you now consider your sentence lengths again, scanning your manuscript for pages where all the sentences or paragraphs are the same length or otherwise overly similar in shape, aiming to see what happens when you start or close paragraphs with simpler, more declarative sentences, instead of long, winding, multiclause, comma-ridden, overly punctuated sentences (like this one). When you can, try to end with a bang.

If your sentences are too similar, you've given up an opportunity to make drama at the level of the prose and, therefore, might be working only at the level of the event. Find every advantage you can to move your reader, to keep them engaged.

Sentence variety is one way of doing this, but it's worth noting that you might also profitably reduce variety for effect: if every sentence in a passage is exactly the same length, or if you employ an unbroken series of one-sentence paragraphs, other pleasing and striking experiences might be created with different kinds of emphases.

Analyze Patterns of Stressed and Unstressed Syllables

In her essay "The Sentence Is a Lonely Place," Garielle Lutz offers a number of suggestions for improving your sentences, including paying attention to the number and location of stressed syllables in your prose. Lutz writes, "Make sure that the stressed syllables in a sentence outnumber the unstressed syllables. The fewer unstressed syllables there are, the more sonic impact the sentence will have," and "Unless you have good reason not to do so, end your sentence with the wham and bang of a stressed syllable . . . Such sentences stop on a dime instead of wavering forward for a wishy-washy further syllable or two."

Not every writer employs this tactic, and it's certainly not a hard-and-fast rule. But it is worth training your ear to notice the stresses in your sentences. Once you've done so, stress and unstress become another instrument you can play. Turning up the stresses in a sentence and cutting back on unstressed syllables—cutting the squishiest adverbs and many extraneous clauses throughout the sentence and especially at the end—can make a sentence feel more solid. Revising with

Lutz's suggestion in mind will help you analyze the choices you've made about how you begin, extend, and eventually exit your sentences. Knowing what you're doing at this heard but mostly unseen layer of language offers opportunities to lead your reader by the ear, using sound in ways both subtle and striking.

Explore Other Syntactical Possibilities

If you're looking to explore more of the possibilities that exist inside your sentences, I highly recommend Virginia Tufte's *Artful Sentences: Syntax as Style*, a dictionary of the possible at the level of the sentence. You'll find plenty of grammatical terminology in Tufte's book you might not already know, including sentence types like the "left-branching sentence," which offers ways of delaying the meat of the sentence to great effect, as in this favorite sentence of mine from Leonard Gardner's *Fat City*:

> In the midst of a phantasmagoria of worn-out, mangled faces, scarred cheeks and necks, twisted, pocked, crushed and bloated noses, missing teeth, brown snags, empty gums, stubble beards, pitcher lips, flop ears, sores, scabs, dribbled tobacco juice, stooped shoulders, split brows, weary, desperate, stupefied eyes under the lights of Center Street, Tully saw a familiar young man with a broken nose.

The simplest version of this sentence—"Tully saw" or "Tully saw a man"—is delayed for fifty words that lay out a crowd of broken men from whom the man Tully sees might be plucked. It's a brilliant long sentence. I don't have any insight into how Gardner composed it, but I can imagine a version where it branches right instead of left, with "Tully saw a familiar man with a broken nose" followed by a long listing of the other people's body parts. That works, too, but I don't think it's as strong. Tufte might label a sentence like this as *syntactical symbolism*, where the syntax of the sentence represents the action being described: we move through the crowd of the sentence as Tully moves through the crowd of men, and we see the man and his broken nose emerge alongside Tully.

I use the Tufte book and others like it in similar ways to how I suggested using writing exercises many pages ago: When I'm feeling stuck or bored with my prose, I get out *Artful Sentences* and read it until I find a surprising sentence shape. Then I go back through my novel draft and look for a place where I might try that shape out, either by revising an existing sentence or by writing a new one. You can do this with any book whose style you admire: Where might a sentence of yours benefit from what you see in the prose of another writer?

Avoid the Most Obvious Pairings of Words

There are certain pairings of adjectives and nouns that come to mind so easily they've fallen below the level of cliché: we use them often in everyday speech, where they rarely catch our attention. Even if no reader will consciously object, they remain unfresh, automatic, default writing. I refuse to use worn, pre-used language if I can, and some of these combinations are exactly that: word pairings used so frequently that they've become frictionless, invisible. To me, their presence in a sentence means I haven't made the language fully *mine*. If I notice one of these combos in my draft, I replace it with something less obviously borrowed:

neatly folded	clenched fists
impossibly blue	shaking hands
pitch black	watery eyes
bright white	weak knees
deep blue	pursed lips
racing heart	infectious grin
sharp gaze	chiseled features
rakish grin	leafy suburb
roaring fire	manicured lawn
easy grace	rustling leaves
tight squeeze	bitter cold

DIALOGUE

Of all the elements of fiction a writer might want to master, dialogue is the one I've struggled with the most, especially in early drafts. Fortunately, it's reasonably easy to scan for dialogue in a manuscript. Take the time to do a pass through your manuscript in which you edit only the dialogue, taking the following into consideration.

Direct versus Indirect versus Summarized Dialogue

Direct dialogue is where you report exactly what a character says; *indirect dialogue* is where you render the substance of the dialogue but not the exact language; *summarized dialogue* is a summary of a longer conversation. As you work your way through your dialogue pass, consider your cocktail of these three kinds of dialogue, what you're using when and why. We don't need a long passage of back-and-forth direct dialogue establishing what time characters should meet for brunch. We usually *do* need to see the crucial confession that breaks open a murder case rendered as directly as possible. If the purpose of a conversation is merely to deliver information, try condensing it as much as possible by converting it into summarized dialogue. Remember that characters don't need to rehash information the reader's already learned, even if one person needs to update another. "The detective told the captain what they'd learned at the slaughterhouse" is as effective as an in-scene recounting of it, up to the point where the captain starts asking questions or offering new information.

You might also usefully vary modes of dialogue to create texture and surprise, similar to how you vary sentence lengths for style. For instance, in this passage from Charles Yu's "Standard Loneliness Package," a character named Deep explains how the emotional transference software the characters use functions:

> "Okay, so, the clients," [Deep] would say, "they call into their account reps and book the time."
>
> He liked to start sentences with, *okay, so*. It was a habit he had picked up from the engineers. He thought it made him sound smarter, thought it made him sound like them, those code geeks, standing by the coffee machine, talking faster than he could think, every word a term of art, every sentence packed with logic, or small insights or a joke. He liked to stand near them, pretending to stir sugar into his coffee, listening in on them as if they were speaking a different language. A language of knowing something, a language of being an expert at something. A language of being something more than an hourly unit.
>
> Okay, so, he said, they book the time, and then at the appointed hour, a switch in their implant chip kicks on and starts transferring their consciousness over. Perceptions, sensory data, all of it. Okay, so, then it

goes first to an intermediate server for processing and then gets bundled with other jobs, and then a huge block of the stuff gets zapped over here, where it gets downloaded onto our servers and then dumped into our queue management system, which parcels out the individual jobs to all of us in the cubicle farm.

The first paragraph is direct dialogue, rendering on the page the exact language Deep uses. The next paragraph mostly isn't dialogue, but it contains a description of *how* Deep speaks, as well as *why* he does so. The third is indirect dialogue, the content of what Deep is saying but not the exact words, except for "okay, so," a speech tag Yu carries over from the previous paragraphs to give the indirect dialogue more texture. It's a skillful transition between modes, saving space while delivering information with more style and voice than straight exposition likely would.

Summarized dialogue creates even more compression, without necessarily giving up style or voice. This paragraph from Don DeLillo's *The Names* employs summarized dialogue to recount the bulk of an argument, speeding through what was likely a crass and hurtful conversation while also rendering it into a higher register:

The argument was long and detailed, with natural pauses, and moved from the street to the terrace, into the house, finally up onto the roof. It was full of pettiness and spite, the domestic forms of assault, the agreed-upon reductions. This seemed the point, to reduce each other and everything else. What marriage is for, according to her. Our rage was immense but all we could show for it, all we could utter, were these gibes and rejoinders. And that we did poorly. We weren't able to take advantage of the clear openings. It didn't seem to matter who got the better of it. The argument had an inner life, a force distinct from the issues. There were surges, hesitations, loud voices, laughter, mimicry, moments in which we tried to remember what we wanted to say next, a pace, a range. After a while this became our only motive, to extend the argument to its natural end.

You can also subvert dialogue conventions to create other compelling effects. In the opening chapter of Laird Hunt's *The Impossibly*, two old friends set out to buy a turkey dinner from any restaurant they can find, something they realize isn't exactly possibly: How many restaurants serve turkey dinners any day but Thanksgiving? The scene begins:

It was a cold night in late November, and he said he would like to have some turkey. I told him that I thought this would take some maneuvering. He said he was willing, if I was, to maneuver. I was. We did. It was an interesting night . . .

No, I am sorry, we do not serve turkey, said yet another man in a white shirt and black vest with just a touch too much oil in his hair.

Yes, but do you *have* turkey?

No, we do not have turkey, I am sorry.

Ah, and while I do believe that you are sorry, I do not believe you do not have turkey, why wouldn't you?

We do not, sir, have turkey, nor do I have for you any explanation.

And all I am asking for is an explanation.

Please leave.

Etc.

We did, finally, and following something a little like the interaction I have just described, get our turkey—they had some, by chance it seemed, in the freezer. Neither of us at the end of eating it entirely believed it had been turkey, but it had been called turkey with maximum enthusiasm by the man whose head John had placed in the sink, and it had been appropriately garnished, so we didn't complain.

Hunt begins with a clipped exchange of direct dialogue, then follows it with a summarized continuation of the conversation and an even more effaced account of the subsequent violence by which the two men finally get served something being called "turkey" by a man who has been nearly drowned in an attack tucked quietly into the middle of a long sentence where it might almost be possible to skim past it. The banal dialogue is rendered directly, while the violence and whatever speech accompanied it is summarized almost to the point of invisibility, creating a strange and discomfiting moment, a dark deed partly played for laughs.

Conversation as Competition

In novels (as perhaps in life), much of conversation is competition, even if only subtly: whenever characters are speaking, they're doing so in pursuit of their own agendas, whether that's extracting information, making a convincing argument, or trying to seem funny or sexy or brave. As you proceed through your dialogue pass, analyze the inherent conflicts in each conversation: What do characters want in this scene? What are they willing to say to get what they want? How are they acquiescing to or resisting the demands of others? How does the tension in the conversation escalate as it progresses, and where are its complications and reversals?

Remember also that people rarely say what they mean, and they often talk over each other without listening. We too frequently are only waiting for our turn to speak, and we do not always wait. Dialogue on the page is not the same as dialogue in life, but one way to make it seem more realistic (if that's the goal) is to try to mimic our omissions and aggressions, our ways of not paying attention fully to what other speakers are saying.

Sometimes clever cuts are enough to make your

dialogue more engaging. In an interview about her novel *Prosperous Friends*, Christine Schutt said, "The trick I've employed in the last five years is to have characters chatter away and then, in the next draft, take out every other line. Oddly enough, the speech has more life, more surprise." I've found Schutt's method to be an invaluable hack for overly ponderous on-page conversations. If a conversation is two pages long, I'll try to cut it in half without rewriting any of the dialogue. Afterward, I'll end up having to adjust some of what remains, but this cutting quickly reduces instances where characters speak too pointedly or respond too directly to each other's questions or accusations, manufacturing the kind of evasions and redirections which serve to make dialogue feel truer to life, tenser, and more conflict-driven.

Diminish Weak Dialogue-Adjacent Actions

One of the challenges of writing compelling conversations is writing the action around the dialogue: What are your characters doing while they're speaking? In many drafts, there's an overabundance of filler actions, a plethora of *sighs* and *smiles* and *shrugs* and *winks*, the occasional eyebrow rise or forehead furrow. There's nothing wrong with an individual use of any of these, but they can flag a spot where the writer hasn't found the right action or description that might more artfully take their place. I'd do a search for every one of these and try to reduce and replace wherever I could, looking to insert more telling action and the kind of character-specific movements and descriptions that will more accurately give dimension to the dialogue.

What you're looking for are details or actions demonstrating the emotional subtext of your character's speech: A character who stares at the floor while saying "I promise to love you forever" might not mean it. Another who admits to a crime while trembling nervously in front of his mob boss employer might've been pressured into his confession, no matter how nakedly he recounts his supposed crime.

If you took my earlier suggestion to cut material from the opening and closing paragraphs of underperforming scenes, I hope you haven't thrown that material away. Take a look at what you have in your cut file and see if any of it might be used to replace the smile/sigh/shrug emoting and gesturing you've just identified. More often than not, interesting gestures and scene details already in your cut material can be tucked around your dialogue to good effect.

FUN WITH HIGHLIGHTERS

Late in the revision process, print off your manuscript and then gather a pile of different color highlighters. (You can also do this on the computer or a tablet, but it's so much more satisfying to do it away from the screen, on hard copy.) Choosing a different color for each of the following categories, use your highlighters to analyze your manuscript and prep yourself for a next round of revision.

Explanations

On your first pass, highlight in one color every sentence in which you explain something. A little explanation is occasionally necessary, but if you find yourself constantly expounding upon what's happening or what the reader should be feeling, then one of two things is likely happening: Either the action on the page isn't sufficiently clear for the reader to understand or feel on their own, which means you need to rewrite it; or else you're overexplaining what a smart and sensitive reader should be able to understand or feel for themselves, in which case you need to cut the explanation and let the scene do its work. (In this case, you're telling on top of showing, which is too much.) Ninety-five percent of the time, an explanation is a scaffold. By the time you're done rewriting, your novel's action should be strong enough to stand on its own.

Backstories

Now, with a different color, do a pass through your manuscript where you highlight every instance of backstory. Then ask yourself: What of this is absolutely necessary for a reader to understand the novel? What is there only because I needed to know it in order to write the book?

My sense is that most novels contain more backstory than they need and, so, run the danger of making every character's psychology a too-neat result of their personal history. Some traumatic or at least formative experience is revealed in the character's past, and then the bulk of the novel entails that past experience playing out in the present, dictating the character's response in scene after scene. This makes characters seem simpler than they might otherwise appear, and it does disservice to the complexity with which you've worked to imbue your protagonists.

Like other kinds of problematic exposition, backstory that *explains* your character can go. Any backstory that *complicates* your character is likely doing better work.

It's also possible to have too little backstory, but this happens so rarely that I wouldn't worry about it. If you've made it this far without writing in an abundance of flashbacks, it's unlikely your novel needs more.

One place to study backstory done well is in the novels of N. K. Jemisin, especially *The Hundred Thousand Kingdoms* and *The Fifth Season*. In the former, almost no backstory appears except where it is revealed by the forward movement of the plot, and there are few info dumps or flashbacks. Yeine, that novel's protagonist, discovers her family's history and the true state of her world by investigation and need, which is revealed in tense, conflict-rich dialogue scenes and in occasional visions that are more mysterious than they first appear. It's a great example of how to manage a complex backstory and world-building exposition without sacrificing forward propulsion.

Weakest Sentences

For your next pass, read your novel paragraph by paragraph, and in every single paragraph, highlight (again, in a color you haven't yet used) the *weakest* sentence. This will take some time, and it may not feel great, but I promise it's worth it! Once back at the computer, do two things: First, delete all these weakest sentences. Second, consider if what remains of the paragraph is strong enough to stand the deletion. Most often it will be, because the weak stuff—especially the kind of weak sentence you've already rewritten a dozen times but never got right—eventually forces the surrounding sentences to make up for its lack. Wherever you feel something is awry in your post-deletion prose, write a new sentence into the deleted one's place instead of continuing to tinker with the broken one.

This is a big job, but the outcome can be dramatic. My novel *Appleseed* contained about 2,500 paragraphs in its final form. If it'd had that number in an earlier draft, and if I had removed the weakest sentence from every paragraph, the novel would immediately have become a lot more concise, and what remained would have been of a higher overall quality.

A variation on this exercise is to let yourself cut only the weakest clause you can find in each paragraph, instead of the weakest sentence. That's a less dramatic operation, but it has a similarly powerful outcome, while also exposing any sentences that are too convoluted or that start early or end late.

Strongest Sentences

On the next pass, highlight (in yet another color) the *strongest* sentence in each paragraph. Now think about why each sentence is stronger than what's around it and what it would take to lift the rest of the surrounding prose to the same level. Why? Because in the end, every sentence should be as strong as possible. By doing this, you'll identify the qualities of your best sentences, and then you can plan how those qualities could be spread to the rest of the manuscript.

Wherever You're Moved

This last highlighting pass might work best on a clean copy of the novel, but it could also be effectively done on a tablet or e-reader. Whatever medium you choose, read carefully through each chapter, trying as best you can to relax and take in the book as your ideal reader might. As you read, highlight any passages where even at this late stage you feel yourself being genuinely moved—by which I mean simply anywhere you feel some kind of emotional, intellectual, moral, or aesthetic jolt, that feeling we get when we're reading a good book for the first time.

Although you're not reading this book for the first time— you might be reading any particular passage for the hundredth time—I guarantee you'll find places to be moved.

Don't intellectualize your reactions yet; just mark them and carry on.

After you've finished reading, go back and reread your highlights. These are the places in your novel where, despite all the time you've spent with these pages, you most feel your own book working on you.

What an incredible joy, what a great feeling to be surprised by your own book!

Enjoy this as long as you can, then study the highlights: Why were you moved? How was that movement generated by what you'd written?

Now ask yourself two more questions:

First (as you continue to revise), how could you make other moments work as well?

Second (if a whole chapter goes by and you didn't experience an inkling of feeling), is there something wrong with the scene? Maybe, maybe not—you have, after all, read these pages so many times. But be honest with yourself before moving on.

CHANGE THE LOOK OF THE BOOK

At some point, you will become absolutely sick of looking at your novel as it appears on the screen. You've been staring at the same basic formatting for years, so many hours of your life spent inside the dull environs of Word or Scrivener or whatever word processing software you're using. I spend so much time in Word that my monitor's screen has burn-in from the gray panels alongside the Page Layout view, and late in the revision process, when I'm working especially long hours, I often think I see the burn-in even when I'm away from the screen.

At this stage, it's likely not ideal to switch software, but you can try to enliven your view in other ways. Change your fonts, which will shift all your line breaks, making your pages look new. Or make the page margins bigger or smaller, which will have a similar effect. Even changing the zoom level slightly can make the book look "wrong," which might be enough to allow you to see it with fresh eyes. The smallest adjustments allow for all kinds of newness. While you're rearranging your screen view, also take a minute to temporarily set the zoom level to something low, like 25 percent. Now study the shape of your novel. Are there parts where it looks thin, where the paragraphs are short; or where it looks thick, where all the paragraphs go on for several pages? This might show you where the novel is out of balance, or it might merely convince you that this is the mode of the novel: it runs thick and thin, and perhaps there are ways to take advantage of that.

Sometimes you need to see the trees, and sometimes you need to see the forest. Mix up the ways in which you interact with the book as often as you can, until you're seeing it from every possible vantage point.

THE READER DOES NOT WANT YOUR LOGIC

Every novel has its own internal logic, which includes not only the cause and effect of the plot's events but also character motivations, symbol systems, the way themes develop, and how the novel's questions get answered. In many novel drafts, a good portion of this logic appears explicitly on the page, because you, the novelist, thought through the logic in real time as you wrote the novel. You needed to know what events meant, so you explained them. You weren't sure what a character was implying when they made some elliptical statement, so you gave an answer.

At this stage, whatever remains of your sense-making logic might feel baked into the prose. You've polished it up, you've made it pretty (or, purposely, appropriately ugly), and you've gotten used to its being a part of the novel's texture.

Unfortunately, that's a problem, because mostly the reader does not want your logic. What the reader wants to do is to connect the dots for themselves, to figure out your characters' motives, to make connections between one scene and another, to explore and solve the mysteries of your novel. If you get in their way by leaving your logic on the page, then you're taking away some of the joy of reading fiction.

Think of it this way: The logic currently on the page is a record of your experience. It's everything you thought and felt and discovered while experiencing the story as you were creating it. Now you've got to clear the board so a reader can have their own experience, making their own journey through the world you've created.

You've already worked on this logic-removing step to some extent, in the highlighting section: this is part of what you cut away while trying to reduce explicit explanations and over-whelming backstory passages. Now you can continue to search for the ways your logic manifests itself inside your sentences.

Consider this passage from the middle of Toni Morrison's *Sula*, where the title character returns to her hometown after a long absence:

> Accompanied by a plague of robins, Sula came back to Medallion. The little yam-breasted shuddering birds were everywhere, exciting small children away from their usual welcome into a vicious stoning. Nobody knew why or from where they had come. What they did know was you couldn't go anywhere without step-ping in their pearly shit, and it was hard to hang up clothes, pull weeds or sit on the front porch when robins were flying and dying all around you.

It's a striking passage, one introducing three new mysteries at once: What is the meaning of this "plague of robins," where has Sula been, and why has she returned? These three myster-ies are linked by being placed in the same sentence, but none explains the others in any straightforward way. Morrison could have written out an explanation, but go ahead and add one for her. It's hard, isn't it? If you appended *because* to any of the sentences just quoted, it would ruin it. The mysteries in this passage can only be hurt by explanation so close to their introduction—and Morrison never does explicitly explain the linking of Sula's return to the plague of robins, leaving it to the reader to make of it what they will.

In your own manuscript, search for obvious logic indicators (there are too many of these to list, but start by searching for *since*, *so*, *besides*, *also*, *although*, *clearly*, and *thus*), including conjunctions like *because*, because wherever *because* appears, it's often followed by your explaining what precedes it. (As in the sentence you've just read.) Most often, conjunctions used this way create clear logical relationships between two ideas—but we're looking to break some of those relationships. Note also that many uses of *and* and *but* make similar logical connections between two clauses or sentences, connections that can often be usefully broken to let two ideas or actions or images rest against each other, creating a little logic gap the reader will have to cross, their mind jumping like a spark between two electrodes. We like this logic-making sensation when we read. We quietly object when it's stolen from us.

CUT EVERYTHING YOU CAN

At some point, I begin to cut everything I can stand to cut: I'm a writer who writes more material than he needs and then trims back. I've learned to trust this part of my process, to look forward to the part where I make the book as tight as I possibly can after living in a baggier, more expansive version of the text. I know I'm not the only writer who does this. George Saunders once talked about his great thirty-five-page story "Sea Oak" being more than one hundred pages long before he "cut out all of the bad stuff." Susan Steinberg, who was a painter before she started writing, says that the process in both mediums is similar. "I first put a lot on the page/canvas," she says, "then scrape most of it off, or pare it down, to get to what I want to say." William Burroughs said that if he had a book of two hundred pages, then you should assume he once had a book of six hundred.

Be merciless when you cut. All that should be left is what you cannot imagine living without—only what applies, what makes the story better.

But don't worry. Nothing you cut is wholly lost on the reader; no effort is wasted. "Even those pages you remove somehow remain," Elie Wiesel once said. "There is a difference between a book of two hundred pages from the very beginning, and a book of two hundred pages which is the result of an original eight hundred pages. The six hundred pages are there. Only you don't see them."

If you're feeling bad about cutting, be grateful you don't work in television. In a Vulture article about HBO's *Veep*, the writer noted that "a typical half-hour of television comedy yields between 12 and 25 hours of raw footage. On *Veep*, because they try so many ways of doing a scene, the range is more like 50 to 80 hours."

Eighty hours of footage to get a thirty-minute show would, if translated into novel-writing terms, be like writing 48,000 pages to get a 300-page novel.

Which isn't to say novelists don't sometimes approach such proportions. In an interview about her second novel, *Inland*, Téa Obreht described how much she had to write to reach her story: "I threw 1,400 pages in the trash . . . It felt like failure a lot. But then I realized it was just a different way of measuring progress, that I was opening doors and realizing there was nothing in the room and then closing those doors and continuing down the hallway."

Inland is 386 pages in hardcover. Obreht wrote five books to publish one, which sounds exhausting and probably was. But sometimes this is how the work gets done.

My first novel was 123,000 words in manuscript, 90,000 words when it sold, and 63,000 words in print. My second novel is 72,000 words in print, but at one point it was double that, plus it had a cut file with another 100,000 words in it. My novel *Appleseed* went out to editors at 135,000 words, after I'd cut 50,000 words from it in the two months before, on top of the other 100,000 words of ultimately unusable stuff I'd written to get to that draft. When I'm reading the final copies of my books, I feel a stronger version of the sensation Elie Wiesel describes than any reader of mine ever will: I remember all the trimmed backstories, all the explanations I cut, all the pairs of characters who got combined into one person, all the detail and research that hit the cutting room floor.

I remember the pages I've cut, but I do not miss them.

What remains is what belongs: only what my ideal reader requires.

SERIOUSLY, REFUSE TO BE DONE

You're so close now! Thanks to all your hard work, your novel might be very good at this point, almost as good as you can make it on your own. You could send it out to agents, you could submit to a publisher, you could certainly give it to friends to read, and likely they would enjoy it nearly as much now as they would if you worked on it a little more first. This is, I know, one of the hardest phases of the project. You're likely exhausted, a bit tired of your novel (if not a lot tired), ready to work on anything else, ready to be done, done, *done*.

Refuse. Refuse to be done. Just a little longer. This is the phase Francine Prose once wrote of as "putting every word on trial for its life: changing an adjective, cutting a phrase, removing a comma, and putting the comma back in." You may never be able to make yourself do it again if you flinch from it now.

My final three suggestions are ways of forcing yourself back into the prose one more time, in the hope of making your novel as tight as it can be before you call it done. After you think you can't possibly look at the manuscript one more time, these three tasks will help you stick with it a couple of weeks longer.

I promise the benefits to your prose will be worth it.

Now, at last, comes the time not to give up on making your sentences *perfect*.

Weasel Words

Gabe Durham, my editor at Boss Fight Books, taught me the expression "weasel words," which Wikipedia in turn explained was popularized by Theodore Roosevelt after first appearing in a short story by the otherwise-forgotten fiction writer Stewart Chaplin, who colorfully described these as "words that suck the life out of the words next to them, just as a weasel sucks the egg and leaves the shell." For me, the term has come to be a catch-all descriptor for the words I might use to get out of writing better sentences: each one is a tiny crutch, a bit of filler prose letting me move my fingers fast over the keys instead of getting bogged down in writing better prose. Some are empty words that can easily be deleted, while others indicate a need to replace some part of a sentence with something stronger.

One weasel word I overuse is *that*, which in some sentences is simply unnecessary—for instance, I could have started this sentence "One weasel word that I overuse is *that*"—and in others still keeps me from writing a better sentence. When I did my weasel word search in the manuscript of my novel *Scrapper*, I deleted eight hundred uses of *that*, none of which would have been a deal breaker for someone reading my book, but that I didn't need and that were, in essence, *three full double-spaced pages* I was unnecessarily making the reader slog through. My book is better off without those three pages of *that*, and yours will be, too.

Here are some other weasel words you might search for, all

of which have their uses but can also indicate opportunities for further revision:

finally	of the	thick
suddenly	once	thin
always	else	strong
sometimes	just	strange
again	merely	weird
even	seem	think
still	large	understand
like	huge	wonder
something	big	know
anything	wide	find
everything	great	very
thing	long	every
mostly	massive	grin
almost	giant	smile
surely	enormous	shrug
perhaps	vast	nod
maybe	tiny	look
at last	small	see
quite	little	watch
then	hard	
and then	soft	
of them	weak	

The best way I've found to deal with an overreliance on any of these is to turn on Track Changes, then do a Find and Replace to delete every instance of one weasel word at a time: this will take out every single *finally* in the book, for instance, with Track Changes and Word's reviewing tools allowing you to consider each deletion. Can the word simply be removed? Or does something more have to be done to fix the sentence?

Some of these words soften an image, making it tentative or provisional: "She seemed like a giant" might become "she was a giant," which feels more solid. Others are the kind of dialogue-adjacent actions we discussed earlier, or thought verbs that don't need to be on the page. Some will be redundant descriptions: a "huge giant," for instance. Others are false attempts at drama: Many manuscripts I saw as an editor were flush with "finally" and "suddenly," falsely trying to make moments more dramatic. But how many things can happen "finally" in any one book?

I'll say it again: I'm a writer who cares deeply about the quality of his sentences, all the way through. But in the last month of work on *Appleseed*, I spent two weeks doing this work through four hundred-plus pages of prose I thought I'd pushed harder than ever before. Soon I'd deleted 201 uses of *always*, leaving 98 behind. I deleted 32 uses of *finally* and all but one use of *suddenly*. Three hundred uses (another full page!) of *still* came out of the book. Fifty *strange* images became 4. A whole page of *just*, gone. A whole page of *so*, 92 uses of *great*, 51 uses of *sometimes*. Nineteen images tagged as *vast* became one, surely vaster now for its uniqueness.

A lot of this would be invisible to readers if left behind: you're never reading a novel and thinking, whoa, too many uses of *still*. But these overuses add up, they slow down the text, robbing it of some of the quality it might have if you replaced your weasel words with better ones, if you fixed your sentences so they didn't need such propping up.

You'll inevitably improve much of the surrounding prose as well. I like to make eliminating weasel words one of the last tasks I perform on a manuscript, because it offers such a sure door back into prose I've been staring at for years by this point.

Before you leave the weasel word process behind, you might ferret out a few more overused words by doing a word frequency analysis, using software to see if you've been employing any odd words too often. We often overuse some unexpected word, an adjective we lean too hard on or a verb we can't get enough of. I was once enthralled by *thrum*, which I've been told can't show up on every page. Take the list you generate, then go through your manuscript using the same method I've just outlined; see if there's anything worth adjusting. Just like with the weasel word list, you're likely to find some sentences in need of late-game tweaking, and you'll reduce the kind of accidental echoes you sometimes find in a novel, where a writer keeps repeating some overly conspicuous word without noticing they're doing it.

Pull Up Your Widows

Another way to refuse to be done is to go through your manuscript and try to remove all the widows from your paragraphs, the one or two or three words dangling onto the next line of a paragraph as it appears on the screen.

I learned this trick from a brief craft essay by Pam Houston, where she said she'd wanted the sentences in her novel *Contents May Have Shifted* to work harder than her sentences had ever worked before:

> So when I got to the 15th, and I believed final, draft, I decided to spend some weeks doing nothing but pulling up "widows." Every time there was a word or two at the end of a paragraph that spilled over to the next line, I found a way to compress the language of the paragraph so that it got pulled "up" to the line above . . . I knew, of course, that the layout of my manuscript would bear no resemblance to the typeset book. This process was simply a way to say to each sentence, "I know you think you're as tight as you can get; now let's tighten you up just a little bit more."

As Houston notes, widows and orphans in your manuscript are completely arbitrary, but eliminating them will force you to make tough choices about sentences you thought you couldn't possibly revise any further. Guess what? You probably can.

You will. And every sentence you find one last way to improve makes for a better novel.

In her essay, Houston says it took four months to do this work to a two-hundred-fifty-page manuscript, during which she cut seventeen pages of prose. That's an incredible tightening of what was already likely a tight manuscript. I've never spent four months doing only this, but every time I try it, I'm awed by how much it improves my prose. It's a simple trick but one of my favorites. And it can be done at any phase of the process, not only at the end: it's useful here as a way of doing *one more draft* when you're as tired of your book as you'll ever be, but I've gotten into the habit of doing it throughout my drafting, tightening as I go.

At the end of this process, I switch the novel's font, which arbitrarily changes the appearance of the text. Then I go through the book one more time, pulling up every new widow I find.

A Celebratory Read, Possibly Aloud

The last thing I do before I send a novel to my readers or to my agent is to read it myself once more. Here I'm trying to experience it as a reader might, trying to enjoy what I've made, to feel proud of the work I've done, the novel I've written. Soon the book will begin to belong to other people: friends and first readers, agents and editors, publicists and booksellers and critics and, eventually, more readers I've never met and mostly never will. But for one more day, the novel's mine—and so, I want to savor, one last time, the feeling of being the only person who has lived inside this version of the world I've made, alongside these characters I've invented.

Still, it's hard to read your book at this point without skimming it or wanting to do anything other than read it again. One way around this is to read the book aloud to yourself. It'll force you to hear every word, every sentence, to stay inside the prose for the hours it'll take you to read it. But it's also a way to make this best version of your novel felt in your body—read with your eyes, given life by your voice, heard by your ears. It's a beautiful gift you can give yourself, before you give the gift of your novel to everyone else.

CONCLUSION

Here's the thing about refusing to be done: one day, you get to stop refusing, you get to be finished with refusal.

One day, the novel you set out to write will be done, and nothing else you do will ever undo that doneness.

Writing a novel and seeing it through to its best possible form is an impressive achievement. Every time I reach the point where I've truly taken a novel as far as I can on my own, I feel simultaneously exhausted and elated, maybe even shocked. I imagine you will, too. Take some time to soak in these feelings before you do anything else. Through an incredible expenditure of effort and imagination and persistence, you've earned this moment. You deserve to bask in its glow.

One of my favorite quotes about the writing life comes from Jane Smiley, who said, "I believe that you either love the work or the rewards. Life is a lot easier if you love the work." I imagine it's obvious by now that I'm the kind of person who truly loves the work. The rewriting and revision tactics in this book are some of the ways I stay inside the process, how I keep it going, how I've learned to make the process into a beautiful thing all its own. I hope you've felt a similar joy and that you know that what happens to you in the time you're at the desk, all the thoughts and feelings and achievements you had there, is what you'll best remember from all the time you spent writing and revising and rewriting your novel.

I wish you the success you desire, and I hope all the dreams you have for your novel come true. But I also hope you feel that what you've already done is something to cherish. We all know that no matter how much rewriting we do, not every novel is going to "turn out"—if "turn out" means get published, or win an award, or sell a million copies. But by the time you find out any of that, much of what novel writing can do for you has already happened. The person you've become while writing your book is one of novel writing's best rewards, and that reward is already yours. No one can take it away, no one can add to it. Don't forget that.

Finally, I hope that whatever helpful tactics you've discovered in this book will remain useful as you press onward. It's my honest belief you'll enjoy every stage of the writing process more as your revision and rewriting habits become more robust. As the tactics in this book stop being something you have to explicitly set out to do, they'll merge with the rest of your everyday suite of abilities, further enabling you to take your writing farther than ever before.

More than likely, you bought this book to write a particular novel. If you've tried most of what's in this book, then by the time you've finished, you'll know you've given that novel everything you can. That alone is worth all the effort described here. To know for sure that you've done your best, that the novel you've written has become the purest expression of its potential you could make it, is an incredible joy.

Celebrate this feeling for as long as you can—and then get ready for the day you decide to do it all over again.

ACKNOWLEDGMENTS

Thank you once again to the entire team at Soho Press, especially my editors, Mark Doten and Rachel Kowal, and my publisher, Bronwen Hruska. This book marks ten years of our working together, and I couldn't be more grateful for our continued collaboration.

Thank you to my agent, Kirby Kim, for all his advice and championing of my work.

Thank you to Sarah Viren and Joseph Scapellato for serving as my first readers, and to David Drummond for his excellent cover design.

Thank you to the innumerable writers whose transparency about their craft informed and strengthened my own. Thank you to my talented students, for their ambition and dedication on and off the page; thanks especially to those in my novel-writing classes at Northern Michigan University and Arizona State University, where much of this book originated.

Thank you to my own writing teachers, and to my colleagues at ASU and elsewhere. A special thank-you to Heidi Lynn Staples at the University of Alabama, who first suggested I turn my traveling craft talk on revision and rewriting into a book.

Thank you above all to Jessica, whose love and support make everything possible.

LITERARY WORKS CITED
AND REFERENCED

Renata Adler, *Speedboat*.

Jane Alison, *Meander, Spiral, Explode*.

Margaret Atwood, *The Testaments*.

Chris Bachelder, *The Throwback Special*.

Nicholson Baker, *The Mezzanine*.

Jesse Ball, *Census*.

Jorge Luis Borges, "On Exactitude in Science."

Robert Boswell, *The Half-Known World*.

Edward Carey, *The Swallowed Man*.

Will Chancellor, *A Brave Man Seven Storeys Tall*.

Jen Chaney, "*Veep* Is Over. Is America Next?" in *Vulture*.

Ted Chiang, "The Lifecycle of Software Objects," in *Exhalation*.

Lucy Corin, "Material," in *The Writer's Notebook*.

Don DeLillo, *The Names* and *Underworld*.

Joan Didion, *The White Album*.

Anthony Doerr, "The Caretaker," in *The Shell Collector*.

Lucy Ellmann, *Ducks, Newburyport*.

Leonard Gardner, *Fat City*.

Garth Greenwell, *What Belongs to You*.

Amitav Ghosh, *Gun Island*.

Amanda Goldblatt, *Hard Mouth*.

Lauren Groff, *Arcadia*.

Pam Houston, *Contents May Have Shifted*; and "On Revision: Pulling Up Widows," in *Hunger Mountain*.

Richard Hugo, *The Triggering Town*.

Laird Hunt, *The Impossibly*.

Marlon James, *Black Leopard, Red Wolf*.

N. K. Jemisin, *The Fifth Season* and *The Hundred Thousand Kingdoms*.

James Joyce, *Ulysses*.

Anna Keesey, "Making a Scene: Fiction's Fundamental Unit," in *The Writer's Notebook*.

Brian Kiteley, *The 3 A.M. Epiphany* and *The 4 A.M. Breakthrough*.

Milan Kundera, *The Curtain*.

Rachel Kushner, *Telex from Cuba*.

Anne Lamott, *Bird by Bird*.

Victor LaValle, *The Changeling*.

Ursula K. Le Guin, *Steering the Craft*.

Clarice Lispector, *The Hour of the Star*.

Garielle Lutz, "The Sentence Is a Lonely Place," in *The Believer*.

Carmen Maria Machado, "Worlds Flipped Sideways," in *Los Angeles Review of Books*.

Peter Markus, *We Make Mud*.

Cormac McCarthy, *Blood Meridian*.

Robert McKee, *Story*.

Toni Morrison, *Sula*.

Flannery O'Connor, *Mystery and Manners*.

Téa Obreht, *Inland*.

Jenny Offill, *Dept. of Speculation.*

Benjamin Percy, *Red Moon.*

Francine Prose, *Reading Like a Writer.*

Joshua Rothman, "The Art of Decision-Making," in *The New Yorker.*

Matthew Salesses, "A Month of Revision," in *Necessary Fiction*; and *Craft in the Real World.*

George Saunders, "Sea Oak," in *Pastoralia.*

Kathryn Scanlan, *Aug 9—FOG.*

Christine Schutt, *Prosperous Friends.*

Jane Smiley, *Thirteen Ways of Looking at the Novel.*

Alexis M. Smith, *Marrow Island.*

Susan Steinberg, *Machine.*

Justin Torres, *We the Animals.*

Virginia Tufte, *Artful Sentences: Syntax as Style.*

Jeff VanderMeer, *Annihilation* and *Wonderbook.*

David Foster Wallace, *Brief Interviews with Hideous Men.*

Jesmyn Ward, *Salvage the Bones.*

Claire Vaye Watkins, *Gold Fame Citrus.*

Joe Wenderoth, *Letters to Wendy's.*

James Wood, *How Fiction Works.*

Virginia Woolf, *Mrs. Dalloway.*

Charles Yu, "Standard Loneliness Package," in *Sorry Please Thank You.*

INTERVIEWS CITED

Nicholson Baker, The Daily Beast.

Robert Boswell, *Hobart*.

Traci Brimhall, NPM Daily.

Kevin Brockmeier, *The New York Times*.

Will Chancellor, *The Rumpus*.

Samuel R. Delany, *The Paris Review*.

Don DeLillo, *The Paris Review*.

Deborah Eisenberg, *The Paris Review*.

William H. Gass, The Daily Beast.

Garth Greenwell, *The Paris Review*.

Heidi Julavits, *Interview*.

Rachel Kushner, *BOMB* and BuzzFeed.

Hilary Mantel, *The New York Times*.

Michael Martone, Powell's.

Téa Obreht, *Time*.

George Saunders, *BOMB*.

Christine Schutt, *Ploughshares* and *TINGE*.

Jim Shepard, *BOMB* and *Memorious*.

Sam Shepard, *The Missouri Review*.

Jane Smiley, *The Atlantic*.

Susan Steinberg, *The Rumpus*.

Amy Tan, The Daily Beast.

Laura van den Berg, *Tin House*.

Claire Vaye Watkins, *Guernica*.

Elie Wiesel, *The Paris Review*.